The Unofficial Biography of
Professor Dr Christopher B Lynch
Written by Nana Ofori-atta Oguntola

Printed in the United Kingdom.

ISBN: 9798468413548

Cover Design: The Printshop

WRITTEN BY NANA OFORI-ATTA OGUNTOLA

Published by VINASHA Productions, A division of World Media Initiatives CIC, United Kingdom

Website: www.worldmediainitiatives.org

Dedicated to:

My children: Daniel, Michael and Esther Oguntola,
My nephews: Israel and Toby Ajakaiye
My godsons: Khartib Stevens and George Davis
May you always remember 'Family is All'.

CONTENTS

FORWARD

The author is a Freelance Writer, Filmmaker and an Event Management Guru. She is CEO of VINASHA Productions and Consultancy, the premier Event Management and film production outfit which is also an award winning production company in the Gambia with a sister company based in the UK.

I met the author during my sojourn in the Gambia when my country Sierra Leone was embroiled in an eleven-year senseless civil war. Initially I had done some stage acting with the Ronko Theatre in Freetown and had worked part time at Sierra Leone's then only broadcasting service. The school at which I was teaching had just won a trophy, after showcasing a play I had written and directed at an inter secondary school drama competition. It was little wonder finding myself as one of the first recruits of the newly established VINASHA Consultancy; a brainchild of the author. To say I learnt a lot during my sting at VINASHA will be an understatement and I also became one of the strongest pillars in the establishment.

On my return to Sierra Leone, I got engaged in full time journalism and I am currently the Managing Editor of the Salone Times Newspaper one of the leading Newspapers in the country and also the current Chairman of the Guild of Newspaper Editors in Sierra Leone.

The book, 'The Professor and I', is a motivational and sentimental masterpiece. It describes the day to day ascent of a child from very humble beginnings to one who rubbed shoulders with royalty. In fact, the lives of Heads of States, the high and mighty and even a member of the British Royal family were left to his medical discretion. The author professionally reaches out to the reading public especially the underprivileged youths who are wary of what the future might bring, bearing in mind the socio-economic challenges not only in Africa but the world over.

What the writer has done to the story is just incredible! Her professionalism enables the reader to grow from stage to stage with the Professor. From start to finish, the author unwittingly transforms the reader into the protagonist where at almost every chapter and page, the reader rejoices or empathises with the Professor at his highs or lows.

I hope this book will ultimately find its way into libraries, classes and lecture rooms to serve as a model for students to realise that hard work pays.

By Donald Theo-Harding.

Editor, Salone Times

1

I WANT TO WRITE YOUR STORY

I met Professor Dr Christopher Balogun Lynch around 2010. I was surprised to hear his story. As a storyteller, I immediately fell in love with his story. My husband had interviewed him for his newspaper column, *The MKMIX* in Milton Keynes, England.

I then followed it up with a video interview at his seven-bedroom home in Great Linford, Milton Keynes. At a gated property, I noticed a main house with garages to the side of the house and a set of flats on top of the garages.

As my husband and I drove to the outhouse he was directing us to I noticed a face peering out of the window of the big house. He later told us that it was his wife keeping an eye on whomever it was coming to see him. The outhouse where we conducted the interview was his consulting office.

Following that interview, the professor grabbed his coat and walking stick and said he had to catch a train as he had an appointment with a lawyer. He said his wife was in the process of divorcing him and she was trying to get a restraining order to stop him from seeing their four children.

My husband and I were quite startled by his revelation, but we made nothing of it and left after filming, talking only about what a nice property he had and what a great man he was.

At home we discussed writing his biography and nominating him to receive a Knighthood. My husband called him and talked to him about it a few days later and he said he would like to speak to his wife first.

That did stun us but again we just thought... *'well, they were married after all, and he probably just wanted to consult with her'*. Then at an appointed time in the evening my husband called him. The professor received the call and passed the phone to his wife. I was sitting on the bed. My husband spoke to his wife then hung up the phone after he said *'OK. Thanks, bye'*. I was all ears to hear what the professor's wife had said.

My husband turned to me *"She said her husband has not done anything worthy of a book or knighthood so she saw no reason why we should be trying to do those things"*.

We were shocked by the response from Professor Lynch's wife and so we shelved the idea and moved on with other things.

Eight years later, influenced by the *Hidden Figures* film which told the story of three black women who helped NASA go to the moon, I decided to create a film project called *Hidden Stories*.

The films were to be produced by young people in Milton Keynes and feature six of the first black professionals to come to Milton Keynes. I received funding from the Heritage Lottery Fund to produce the project.

Of course, Professor Lynch came to mind straightway as one of the founders of the Gynaecological Ward at Milton Keynes Hospital. One of the films produced by the young people focused on him.

The project was featured on BBC News and Professor Lynch was interviewed on both the breakfast and evening news.

On the day his story was aired on TV, I went to see him and asked him if he had seen himself on TV that morning. He hadn't, but his daughter told me her mother, who was now his ex-wife had seen the news and called and told her about it. I informed him he would be on TV that evening as well.

Following the premiere of the films in the *Hidden Stories* project, which Professor Lynch attended, and which was also attended by the young filmmakers, their families, the Mayor, other people featured in the project and guests, I approached Professor Lynch to ask him if I could write his autobiography.

The Professor decided that I could write the biography. So, the project to write down his autobiography started in earnest and became a major part of both our lives from November 2018 to February 2020.

There was no money to fund the project, so we created a 'Go Fund Me' account and invited over seventy of the Professor's friends to support the project. The Professor and I were very optimistic that with the number and calibre of people he knew, had worked with or had helped we would meet our target of £45,000.

We ended up receiving £6000 pounds in donations, £3000 of which was paid to me as my fee for the work done on the autobiography for almost fifteen months.

I was disappointed that I was not receiving a bigger fee. However, I had my eye on the bigger prize, which was to ensure the story of Professor Lynch was written and made available for posterity. I also felt the sales from the book and the ultimate aim of turning his story into a film would more than make up for the paltry initial fee. He said I was too optimistic and even though he did not say it, I could sense he was also disappointed.

When we started, I provided the professor with a small video camera so he could take his time to narrate his life story. He had already written down the sections under which he wanted to divide his narration.

At the start of this project, he had been diagnosed with prostate cancer and I was worried he might not make it through and thus lead to an unfinished book. Though he suffered fatigue every day after his treatment, he still managed to keep dictating his thoughts throughout this period.

As a member of the masonic society, he had risen to the rank of Grand Deacon of Grand Lodge and was a senior member of his group in the St Giles Lodge in Milton Keynes.

One day the Lodge was offering free blood tests for Prostate cancer to all its members. Professor volunteered to have a test done even though he was asymptomatic. The test, unfortunately, came back positive. His GP referred him to the urologist at Milton Keynes Hospital.

After the initial test, he was subjected to a number of more rigorous tests and they found he had developed cancer.

He found the news devastating. He thought it was the end of his life. Being a doctor, made it even harder to accept because he was more used to giving bad news to patients and somehow failed to expect it would happen to him. Fortunately, it was confined to the Prostate and hadn't evaded its capsule or spread. His bone scans were all normal showing no signs of metastatic disease.

His treatment was hormone injections every three months and radiotherapy for seven weeks.

The radiotherapy centre was local in Linford Wood in Milton Keynes. He found it ironic that most of the women at the treatment centre had once been his patients. He felt the experience humbled him as previously he was the all-knowing Consultant that patients looked up to and now, he was the patient.

He underwent his seven weeks of radiotherapy and was lucky to get through without any problems, apart from bladder difficulties which are expected of this type of treatment. He described the experience of going through radiotherapy every day as 'hell'.

He found working on his autobiography at the same time as undergoing treatment difficult to do. He said he was exhausted and the thought of returning home every day to do his dictation was just tiring. But he did it and his tests for cancer after his treatment came back as negative.

The cancer did not spread, and he is cancer free which is good news.

I was at his home an average of five times a week to pick up a new narration and discuss the narration I had edited the day before.

Each time I collected the hard drive from the camera I had left him to record his narration I would transfer it onto my computer, then I would wake up at 4am to transcribe the narration.

I had bought software that allows you to narrate into the microphone and it automatically transcribes for you but it did not work too well so it was the traditional listen and write method for me.

As I transcribed, I also edited his narration for grammar and coherence. At about 10am I would then take the edited material to him to look at and make sure that it was true to his words and intentions. Together we would edit the transcript.

I would ask for clarifications or probe him for more details about something he had said and I would go back and re-edit. I would then collect the next tape and that was how we progressed.

This was how I worked with the professor for about eight months before I hired an editor to take the draft copy and start work on finishing the book.

2

HIS BEGINNINGS

Professor Lynch was born in a town called Kabala, in the north of Sierra Leone, West Africa. He is the son of the late Reverend Prince Lynch and Adeoga Dixon.

According to him, his mother was a descendant of Ethiopia, originally from the Falasha tribe who were supposed to be the 12th tribe of the Kingdom of Israel but never recognised as such. He said she had beautiful Fulani features.

His parents both attended and met at Fourah Bay College in Freetown. Fourah Bay College was a college extension of Durham University in England and the oldest university in West Africa.

His father had studied Hebrew, Greek, and Religion, whilst his mother studied English.

He said his father thought his mother was pretty and he liked her immediately. She gave a lot of resistance to dating him, it seemed, because so many other boys were trying to court her.

Despite the competition, she fell in love with his eloquence because he was good at expressing himself and she was impressed with his use of the English Language.

After his parents got married, his father was commissioned to work for the Church Missionary Society in Sierra Leone by Bishop Holstead, an English Bishop sent to oversee the Church in West Africa.

Bishop Holstead took his father under his wing to assist him with sharing his Christian faith.

The professor recounted a story he said his father told his brother Julius, his sister Princess, and himself when he was around five years old. The story was that at that time, his mother was thirty-eight weeks pregnant with him and anaemic, so she was always falling asleep.

His mother had wanted to relax at home rather than accompany his dad that day as he had gone to the local church to officiate the Sunday service. She had fallen asleep in front of the house.

When his father came home around midday, he found her lying on the grass with a snake on her stomach. Alarmed, he made some noise which woke his wife up and startled the creature and thankfully it fled.

He said that as children, his siblings and himself found the story funny. They giggled, saying, *"mummy had a snake on her belly."* They did not understand the seriousness of the issue or the probable disaster that could have taken place. He said that now, of course, he looks back on the situation differently.

The next-door neighbour - who was a chief and had lots of wives - organised the workers to see if they could find the snake. Based on the description, the chief identified the creature as a boa constrictor. Unfortunately, they couldn't find it, but his mother was so traumatised by the experience, she went into labour that very night.

According to Professor Lynch his mother, who was thirty-five years old at the time, had received her pregnancy care from the village nurse as there was no modern antenatal care at the time.

She delivered Professor Lynch at home under the supervision of a birth attendant and suffered severe haemorrhage, which coincidentally, later became his calling and specialty.

His mum had post-partum haemorrhage and so the birth attendant put a hot sandbag on her stomach which compressed the uterus so it could contract down. Despite advances in antenatal care, this is basically the same technique still used today.

He said his father panicked as he thought his new-born child wouldn't survive, given all the traditional medicine which included coconut water they gave the baby to drink and the herbal treatment he received. However, both he and his mother pulled through.

It is an interesting coincidence that he later became a specialist in haemorrhage control, a similar technique to the one which saved his mother's life. Also the snake is an emblematic symbol of medicine. Perhaps, serendipity or providence was setting up a picture of his future without anyone realising it at the time.

His brother Prince then came along followed by his sister, Princess with less drama.

Professor Lynch got on well with his siblings even though, he said, his younger brother used to annoy him by telling people that he was older because he was physically bigger in size. This disrespectful behaviour from his younger brother, he said, caused a lot of sibling rivalry and fights between them especially when he tried to boss him around.

As children they liked animals and his favourite toy was a scooter which he enjoyed speeding down the hill on. He said he fell many times and sustained injuries because the roads had uneven surfaces. His favourite game was playing football with his brother and their neighbours.

Professor Lynch said his maternal grandfather was a goldsmith, originally from Ethiopia. His name was Josephus and they used to call him Grandad Joseph. Professor Lynch used to help him blow the bellows with which he used to turn precious metals into shiny bangles and other trinkets to sell.

He stated that his paternal grandfather worked in a scientific programme with doctors from Cambridge who were working on the tuberculosis vaccine. Their work involved recruiting patients from remote villages who had a chronic cough with Tuberculosis sputum.

There were a lot of deaths from tuberculosis causing the urgent need to find a vaccine. Unfortunately, his grandad died from TB himself.

Professor Lynch told me that when he was old enough, he was taken to start his education at the Holy Trinity Infant School from where he progressed to Sierra Leone Grammar School, which was founded in 1845 and is one of the oldest schools in Africa.

The school was founded in Freetown to provide education to returning slaves after the abolition of slavery. Freetown, the capital city of Sierra Leone, was the centre for the repatriation of slaves from England, the Caribbean, and America. The school provided high quality education and was famous for having students from all over Africa attending it.

He said that as the son of a priest, he did not pay any fees - this was a great help because clergymen didn't earn a lot of money in those days. They were given scholarships till the end of the fifth form.

Professor Lynch describes his dad as being talkative. He loved to win arguments and his favourite phrase was, 'You see, I floored him'. He said as a child he did not understand what that meant but he felt proud of his dad because it meant he had won an argument.

His father died in 1949 when Professor was five years old. Professor Lynch describes his passing as one of the tragedies of his life.

On one Saturday morning Professor and his dad were playing chess. His dad allowed Professor to beat him at chess because he knew the young boy was like him and did not like losing. They finished their game of chess and sat there just talking and laughing when the phone rang.

It was his father's friend who was a bank manager, Mr Derrick Petters. This is the same Mr Petters who later became Professor Lynch's boss when he started working at the bank.

The bank manager friend asked his father if he would go and do some hunting and shooting in Leicester Peak. Leicester Peak was one of the finest reserve areas to go to on a Saturday morning.

After some hesitation, his dad agreed to go with him. That same evening, the two men had planned to attend a dinner club attended by professional people. They would normally go and hunt the meats they would eat at the dinner, like pheasants or wild boar.

He told his friend his car was not working well. Derrick, of course, being a bank manager had a 4x4 which could go through any terrain and offered to pick him up.

His mother left for the market with Professor's brother and sister whilst Professor joined Mr Petters and his dad to go hunting.

Derrick used to hunt in the UK, so he had a gun which was an up and down bow. Professor's father used to hunt and he had a side by side bow.

Professor sat in the back of the Land Rover whilst the two men were talking in the front. Derrick was telling him about his time reading philosophy and economics at Cambridge.

From the back seat, Professor enjoyed their debate and discussion. They matched each other well. His father used to say, *'he may be a Cambridge graduate but I floored him'.*

They arrived at Leicester Peak which was a savannah-like terrain with all sorts of creatures around. They usually hunted wild boar and pheasants. Unfortunately, on this day there were no wild boars, only pheasants in large quantities.

They were difficult to shoot as they ducked and dived easily. The hunt began and there were other huntsmen around.

His father was complaining that his gun was heavy. But this was the same gun he had always used. The rebound was hurting his chest. Still, they had a good time. As a small boy Professor picked up the pheasants which were shot.

After the hunt, Derrick took the pheasants to the chef and told him unfortunately this was all they could shoot. When Derrick dropped them off, his mum and siblings were not yet back home. So, Derrick and his father agreed to meet up for the dinner and Derrick left.

His father felt tired out by the day's activities. He went to lie down on the settee in the front room. Professor was tired as well, so he lay next to him on the settee. After a short while, his brother, sister and mother returned.

His mother had a bird-like whistle which she made to signal she had returned. Professor Lynch said it sounded as if the bird they had gone to shoot had come back to haunt them. But she had no reply from this whistle.

When she came in, she saw Professor lying in front of his dad. She shouted 'Prince, Prince'. Professor woke up and turned round to shake his dad to wake him up. *Unfortunately, there was no response, he could not be roused.*

The next-door neighbour was a doctor so his mum told him to go and get Dr Johnson. He was home in his pyjamas, even though it was in the afternoon. He rushed in and tried to revive him but to no avail.

When his mum realised he was gone, she was devastated. There was utter pandemonium. She was confused, not knowing what to do. His mother rang Mr Petters with whom he had gone hunting.

That evening, Derrick announced to the rest of the dining club that his father had died but he insisted the function should not be upset. So, they went ahead with the dinner on his father's behalf.

The Bishop had an appointment with Professor's dad and was supposed to see him in the afternoon for a meeting. When the Bishop arrived for the meeting, he was informed he had died. The body was still at home then. Bishop Holstead, who was also the Bishop for West Africa, was quite shocked and sad indeed.

The funeral was arranged for the following Saturday, a week later. It took place at the church where he was going to be ordained as a clergyman in Leicester Peak, close to where they went hunting for pheasants.

'This was my first experience of tragedy and I will never forget it' said Professor Lynch.

Professor Lynch described his father as being quite an active person and he learnt later he had died of hypertension and kidney problems. He was forty-two years old when he died.

When I asked him how he felt about his father's death he said he had found it difficult to deal with because he did not understand the full impact of it. He had cried because he had lost a father but he did not mourn because he hadn't known him for very long.

He added that the loss of his dad at such a young age was probably why he spoils his own children and gives them everything they want.

After his father's death, he said his mother became a seamstress. Despite her degree in English, she preferred sewing to teaching as it was more profitable. She made dresses for christenings, confirmations and weddings.

Professor said that when his father died, he left him, aged five, his brother aged three, and his sister aged two to the responsibility of his mother, Mrs Jane Adeoga Lynch.

His father's sister, Mrs Princess King-Ray was much older than him. She was married to a Nigerian academic who was very successful, and they lived in the eastern part of Freetown near his two schools: The Holy Trinity Boys School and The Sierra Leone Grammar School.

His aunt offered to take him from his mother to reduce the burden on her, especially since she had the two younger ones.

Professor Lynch describes his aunt as a successful teacher and happily married.

She and her husband had no children of their own and had adopted a child from Kabala called Kelleh Mansaray who was about eleven or twelve when Professor was five. Kelleh had already been living with the Professor's uncle and aunt in Freetown when he went to live with them.

He adapted to living and being brought up by his aunt and not his own mother. He said it was fun living with his aunt and her husband, but he had constant fights with Kelleh who was bent on making himself the favourite of his adoptive parents.

He said each time he and Kelleh went out, Kelleh would leave early and go home whilst he might go and play football. He realised the reason he left early was to present himself to his aunt and uncle as a more caring boy. Professor would arrive later and often get flogged for coming home late.

The Professor said that one day he squared up to Kelleh and asked:

'Tell me my dear Kelleh, why do you always put me on the spot as though I do not care for my aunt and uncle?'

Professor did not feel Kelleh gave him a sensible or reasonable answer. He felt Kelleh wanted to have the one-upmanship of the two and gain favour with his aunt and uncle which he successfully did.

The Professor said he was more academically inclined than Kelleh was and he sat and passed the secondary school entrance exam, which gave him a scholarship to the Sierra Leone Grammar School. Kelleh, on the other hand struggled through his second school exam but made it in the end with a certificate which took him to a training course in Engineering.

When his uncle sadly died, he said Kelleh got closer to his aunt doing all her shopping and other things making Professor Lynch look like he didn't care as much.

In time, Professor finished his secondary school which led him to working in a bank and later moving to England.

His mum kept in constant touch by visiting him regularly and he spent weekends with her and his siblings.

Kelleh was still living with his aunt after he made his way to the UK. When the Professor left for England, his aunt made some financial deals with Kelleh. This led her to put up her house as security in order to help Kelleh in his enterprises.

She eventually sold the house to finance Kelleh's projects related to his engineering business. With part of the proceeds from the sale of the house, Aunt Princess paid to go on holiday to the United Kingdom for about a month. She lived with Professor Lynch and the Rev MGM Cole during that time. She died a few years after returning home.

The Professor said of his aunt: *'She did look after me well. I must give her what is her due. I would thank her for all she did for me following my father's death when my mother was unable to take care of three children on her own'*.

3
PRELUDE TO UK

Talking about his time at school, Professor Lynch said that to his family's dismay at the time, he had developed an interest in dancing and sports. They did not think these would enable him to bring up a family properly.

Back then, these were not professions which earned a decent living to feed a family or earned respect in society. If you were not a doctor or a lawyer, you were nothing by social standards.

He noted that he was not deliberately rebelling against his parents, it was just a social response to his environment. Sports were part of the school programme which he enjoyed and was good at.

He added: *'And in those days, if you were a good dancer you increased your chances of getting a girlfriend. The girls loved great dancers, so it had obvious appeal. That is exactly how I got my girlfriend, Monica, who was one of the prettiest girls in the school'.*

He said that like his mother, he was also good at English. His Grammar School was designed on the Eton and Harrow system of schooling with speech days, sports days, and a debating society — all very British activities.

They also had the annual house competitions. He was in Quattus House, the other houses were Primus, Secundus, Tershus, and Quintus - all named in Latin.

Professor said he was the head of his house and took part in sports and dance activities. Keen on doing British ballroom dancing, he used the instructions of the well-known dancer Victor Silvesta. Instead of reading textbooks, he'd be reading dance books and so he was considered an authority on ballroom dancing.

He said he also carried around *The Oxford Book of English Verse* which had fine expressions and language quotes, which he used to quote to court Monica.

She was in a boarding school for girls called Methodist Girls' High School. He said his letters to her were flowery and interesting. She used to have fun reading them in her dorm room with her friends. They had nicknamed him *'Shakespeare'* because of the way he wrote his expressions of love for Monica. He said those expressions were genuine though.

Once he finished fifth form, the support from the church for his fees as the son of a clergyman ended. He could not afford to attend sixth form, so he had to do something to supplement his family's income. He applied to Barclays Bank in Sierra Leone who were offering cadet training.

He was seventeen when he applied and the English bank manager at the time, Mr Petters, interviewed him and was impressed with all his extracurricular activities - dancing, sports, and debating.

Mr Petters' wife used to be a dancer in the UK before she joined him in Sierra Leone. Mr Petters was also a friend of his late father and had been the last person, apart from Professor Lynch, to see him before he died.

He offered him the job, as a trainee with a trial period, which he accepted.

He started as a trainee banker and became friendly with Mr Petters. Professor took him to the nearby villages to hunt animals because Mr Petters was a man who loved those British pursuits. At weekends, Professor Lynch would go and see him and his family for a meal which he felt was a good opportunity for him to socialise.

He said Mr Petters encouraged him to make banking his profession, so he enrolled on a correspondence course with two colleges in the UK: one was the Metropolitan College and the other was the Rapid Results College.

The banking qualification was in two parts. The first part of the exam was English Law, British Constitution, Maths and Economics Theory and Practice.

He had already done well in his O'levels in English so he took the first part of the banking diploma exam within six months which he passed and became a Part One Qualified Banker.

Around the same time his girlfriend, Monica whom he had been in love with since high school, told him her father hoped to send her to the UK to study nursing.

The Professor said her father felt that he might get her pregnant, so he wanted to send her far away from him. He said that news broke his heart because it meant separation from the love of his life.

Professor began to make plans to ensure he joined her in the UK the moment she told him the news. He set up a group of colleagues in the bank to make a monthly deposit of money by each member. The total sum of the money would then be collected by one member of the group each month.

Each one in the group would have a turn at receiving the total money collected at the end of the month. This informal self-help financial system is called an *Osusu* in Creole and is still practised in many parts of Africa as a collective saving and money raising method.

He hoped to be the last recipient to draw down the money so he could travel and meet his girlfriend in the UK.

Professor Lynch said in the early days of Monica's travel to the UK he was receiving regular letters from her. As time went on, however, they stopped being as romantic as they used to be. That caused him a bit of concern as he feared she may have made new romantic acquaintances in the UK. After all, she was extremely pretty and desirable.

He resigned from the bank, left Freetown and travelled to the UK on a boat called the *MV Apapa*. The trip lasted ten days at sea which was very rough. There were times when the waves were high and the boat would feel like it was being lifted into the air. It was horrible and he said he felt seasick on several occasions.

It stopped in Liberia, Ghana and Nigeria to pick up more passengers before going to the UK. The Professor met a chap who was a student, Mr Segun Akinluiy. He joined the boat in Nigeria and they became good friends and travelled together.

4

SHOCK HORROR

Professor Lynch told me that he and his new friend, Mr Segun arrived on board the boat, *MV Apapa* at Liverpool docks on an extremely cold day on the 22nd of December 1964.

They were surprised because they expected it to be warm like it was back home. They had light clothes on which were totally unsuitable for the cold. They were shivering and their teeth were clattering. He could not believe it was possible to be this cold. He felt it would all be worth it, however, once he saw his girlfriend again.

They had to get a train to reach their respective destinations. The station master said to them, *"you boys look so cold, you are shivering, why don't you go and buy yourselves some warm clothing"*.

Professor Lynch said he only had fifty-one pounds, two shillings and six pence in his pocket but his Nigerian friend had more money because he came from a richer family.

The station master pointed out a shop across the road called the *Army and Navy Store*. They sold a lot of clothes and things which could be bought for very cheap because they were all donated by retired army, naval and air force personnel.

The Professor said he bought an air force coat and Segun bought an army coat which was also quite heavy. They decided to buy two pairs of boots which were lined with fur to keep their feet warm. The Professor said he still has the coat he bought that day.

That, for Professor Lynch, was the first disappointment of coming to the UK: the sudden change of weather from what they had been used to in their home countries was extreme.

The Professor said his girlfriend, who had come before him and for whom he had made the journey to England, met them at the railway station with a chap who looked like her boyfriend.

The man was well dressed and wore a heavy coat and a bowler hat. He looked sophisticated. Professor said Monica said to him, *"Christopher, it's nice to see you,"* but there was no welcoming hug or love or affection.

Not knowing what England was like, he said he was resistant to being too forward so he held himself back, even though he was disappointed. He added that she said to him, *"Mummy said she's given you some things for me, can I have them please?"*

He felt she spoke in a posh way which was different from the way she spoke when they were in Freetown. She now said *'Mummy'* instead of *'Mama'*.

So, he said to her, *'Look Monica, this is Liverpool Station, it's very cold, I don't have time to open cases and bring things out for you'*. She agreed and asked him where he would be staying so she could collect the items from him later.

She gave him her number and they parted company and she went away with the man who had accompanied her, while he and his friend boarded the train from Liverpool Street Station aiming to get to Euston.

When I asked the professor how the encounter with Monica at the station made him feel he said, *'I was devastated by what had just happened with Monica. I had come all this way on a boat. Endured a very unpleasant trip with sickness and arrived in an extremely cold country, all for Monica to leave me at the station and go off with another man'*.

When we completed the autobiography and placed it on Amazon Monica read the blurb which mentions this experience. I guess she did not like it because she called the Professor whilst I was in his house and though I could not hear what she was saying she was yelling and she sounded cross.

When the phone call ended, I asked the Professor who had called and what was wrong. He said it was Monica and she wanted him to remove the story about her and her male escort from the book. She said Professor Lynch could not say he was her boyfriend because he did not know that for sure. I asked the Professor if I should remove that story from the book but he said *'no'*.

I had met Monica a few years prior to working on the autobiography. She had accompanied Professor to an African event in at Campbell Park in Milton Keynes. I asked her who she was and she said she was Professor Lynch's friend from a long time ago before he married his wife. She insinuated she'd been set aside by Professor in preference of his ex-wife. I was impressed that they had found their way back to each other after so many years.

Years later after I finished writing the biography, I met a Sierra Leonean woman who told me Monica was the lady who had been dumped by Professor Lynch in preference for his white ex-wife.

I am assuming this is the version of the story Monica told people and was not happy he was telling a different one and that was why she wanted it out of the book.

When Professor Lynch's son, Joshua tried to stop the publication of the autobiography he cited Monica's displeasure with her mention as one of the reasons the book had to be unpublished.

Back to the Professor's arrival in the UK: On the train from Liverpool docks, the Professor said they asked some other commuters to let them know when they arrived at Euston. Sitting close to them were a Scottish family.

Their children were running around the train. He said when the children saw them with their big coats – *'me looking like an airline pilot and my friend Segun looking like an army general - they were intrigued.'* He said the boys were looking at them sheepishly and whispering to their mother. One of them came over and tried to pinch his hand to see how he would react but he was pleasant and said, *"Hello, how are you?"*

When the family realised the Professor and his friend could speak English, a conversation started up between them. One of them asked if they would like some coffee or tea. There was a shop on the train and they went and bought them tea and coffee which was kind. He said conversation with them, however, was quite difficult as they had a Scottish accent which he and his friend found difficult to understand.

When the Scottish family left the train at Birmingham, they exchanged addresses and promised to be in contact. The Professor said he did visit them on New Year's Day the following year in Birmingham and stayed with them for three days. It turned out the Scottish believed if they were visited by a black person on New Year's Day it would bring them good luck.

I asked Professor Lynch if he felt offended by that statement and he said because he had not lived in the UK long enough and had not assimilated the negative connotations people could associate with this, he did not mind at all. In fact, he took it as a compliment.

He added that lo and behold, the father did win the Littlewoods Lottery whilst he was there. They felt it was his presence which had brought them good luck. They entertained him but did not give him any part of the money.

His friend, Segun was going to stay in a place called Brixton with a relative and his family whilst the Professor was going to stay in Streatham with his father's friend who was a vicar. When they arrived in Euston, they asked the best way to get to these two places and were given the number of the bus they should take. It was Bus 99 to Brixton.

They got on a double-decker bus but decided to stay on the first deck to avoid the cold. The conductor was kind and let them know when they reached their destination.

His friend gave him his number so they could stay in touch before he left the bus. Professor said he and Segun Akinluiy are still in touch, fifty-five years after they met on the *MV Apapa* from West Africa to the United Kingdom. Segun achieved a PhD in Classics and was once the Ambassador for Nigeria to Paris and is married with children.

When Professor Lynch got off at his destination bus stop, there was a church next to it. He saw an Englishman who looked like a vicar wearing a dog collar with his suit coming out of the church. He got into his car and started to drive off. He waved him down and he kindly stopped.

On telling him he had just arrived from Sierra Leone and was looking for Reverend Cole, the English gentleman told him he knew the Reverend whom everyone called *Speedo* because he was a good footballer. As it happened, he only lived around the corner so he took him to Reverend Cole's house.

When Reverend Cole came to the door Professor Lynch showed him the letter from his mother. It was a request to house him as he was coming to the UK to study.

After the gentleman had gone, the Reverend Cole took him into the house and introduced him to his two sons and daughter who also welcomed him kindly.

The Professor describes Reverend Cole as a pleasant man. His wife was also friendly and he called her Aunt Aida. His daughter who was the eldest was Ekundayo. His first son was Christopher and worked as a lab technician. His second son was Ayodele, a trainee mechanic.

Professor Lynch said the house seemed posh to him as he did not have the luxuries they had back home. It was also warm and welcoming. His room was heated with paraffin heaters, and he had to be careful not to get burnt or start a fire in the house.

He was given a room on the ground floor and it was made clear, it was a rental and not a gift. He would have to pay ten pounds every week. For him, it was a lot of money at the time as it meant he could only stay there for up to five weeks before his fifty pounds would run out. So, he asked the Reverend if there were any jobs in the area he could do.

He gave him a magazine called *The Exchange Mart*. It was a weekly advertiser of jobs and items for sale, which he spent the weekend looking through.

The Professor said he remembered the experience being a bit of a shock to him. He was excited however, about the prospect of being in England. The fact that he had made it to the UK at last overshadowed all the negativity. He was optimistic and excited to get on and make something of his life.

Reverend Cole's daughter who was a nurse cooked them food. He found out he had to make a contribution towards the food as well every week. She was pleasant and gave him advice about living in England. *'What sort of advice?'* I asked the Professor. He said, *'things such as avoid walking alone at night, if you are out on your own, keep to yourself, and avoid street gangs'*.

The Professor felt it was a good household, but everyone kept to themselves. It was not like in Sierra Leone where people mingled freely with each other. Here everyone stayed in their rooms, so it was not as sociable as he was used to, but they were friendly to him.

He said he could rarely contact his mother because phoning home was expensive so he would write letters about his experiences in England. She would write back and also send him things when someone she knew was coming to England.

He describes his first letter to her as comprehensive as he narrated his entire journey and how he was received. He said his mother and siblings were concerned about his safety in England as it was the first time he had travelled so far from home.

Looking at the jobs in the magazine, he saw a job working in a paint factory and he remembers it was called *Cock Chimney Works*. It was about two miles from where he lived but he could not afford the transport to go to work.

There was a next-door neighbour who sold bicycles and made repairs so he went and asked him if he could use a bike to get to the factory. He agreed he could borrow one but if he got the job, he would have to buy it. The Professor never did say if he bought the bike.

He cycled to the factory on Monday and met the manager whose name was Mr Bamfarce. He felt that Mr Bamfarce thought that because he was African, he was strong enough to work outside in the factory grounds loading and unloading paint.

The job was to use forklifts to place tins of paint on to the lorry. The first question they asked was whether he could drive. He told them he could but not the kinds of machines they had and so he was shown how to use them. The Professor said on his first attempt in moving the paint, he watched in horror as all the paint tins fell off. Luckily, they were sealed and didn't spill although some of the cans were dented.

When he went to the foreman's office to explain he had dropped the paint, he was nervous. He was sure he would not get the job. Mr Bamfarce was sympathetic, however, and despite the accident, he offered him the job which he accepted gladly.

Professor Lynch remembers being strongly monitored by Mr Bamfarce when they were working so there was no time wasting. He said he always carried his clipboard to keep a record of where and what everyone was doing all the time.

It was winter and despite the gloves, his hands really hurt as a result of the cold. There were no other black people working in the factory, as it was such an unpleasant climate. The Air Force Coat he had bought on arrival, however, proved useful.

He rode his bicycle every day from Pendle Road where he lived to and from work but as there was ice on the ground at this time of the year, he often fell over.

His big winter coat protected him from getting too many bruises. There were no helmet laws in those days, so he said he would protect his head with his hands. Then he would get back up and continue his ride to work.

He told Mr Bamfarce about his constant falling and he informed him that there was a man who lived close to his house that could give him a lift to work so he didn't have to keep riding in the cold.

The man was an Englishman called Mr Stratfield. He asked him if he could give him a ride to work. He charged him £1 for the journey - in one direction, another expense he had to pay. He would take him to work and bring him back home, as long as he was not doing overtime.

He had to do overtime as he needed the extra money at the time. It worked out well in the end as he could afford to pay Mr Stratfield the extra money to wait for him and take him back home from the overtime work.

Then came the issue of his studies. Professor Lynch had left home with nothing but a Bankers Part One Certificate. He asked Reverend Cole what qualifications he needed to go to University in the UK. He said he needed to have A' Levels.

So, the Professor wrote to the Rapid Results College and the Metropolitan College to continue his correspondence studies with a change of address from the one in Sierra Leone to his new home in England.

He wanted to study law when he came to England and not continue with banking. He noticed from the syllabus that he would have to do English Law, Economics, and British Constitution. This syllabus in England was similar to what he had done in Sierra Leone. He had already done English at O' Levels and Maths as part of the banking exam.

The Professor's former headmaster at the Sierra Leone Grammar School had told him his son was a teacher at King's School, Canterbury. He had given him a letter and said if he ever needed help with his education, he could contact his son and he might be able to help. His name was Johnathan Woods.

Professor Lynch said after seeing the syllabus to prepare for the A' Level exams and everything required, he contacted Mr Woods because he could not afford to go to night school or take on anything that would cost money.

He said when he contacted Mr Woods, he enthusiastically invited him to meet his family because his father had already recommended him. The Professor asked him for help with his studies and Mr Woods assured him that would not be a problem.

Since Professor Lynch lived far from Mr Woods, he could only go to his house for help with his studies on weekends. This meant a loss of income from his weekend work but the exams were due to come up in June so he was willing to give that up.

Professor Lynch took four subjects in A' Levels – English Law, British Constitution, Maths and Economics - all of which he passed with A grades.

Everyone, including Reverend Cole, could not believe how a boy who had only been in the UK for about six months could do so well in his exams. He said they didn't realise he had done banking in Sierra Leone and so was familiar with the subjects.

He said that in fact, the level of work he had done in Sierra Leone was of a higher standard than the ones he had encountered in the UK exams. That, coupled with the help he received from the teacher in Canterbury, helped him through the exams despite the difficult times he was encountering financially.

Going back to Monica, whom he described as 'the reason for my coming to England,' she was living in Bolton. He said she rang him up and said she wanted to come and collect her parcel which her mum had sent.

When she arrived, she came with the same man he'd met her with at the docks, in his big car. The Professor said he thought *'the man looked so arrogant, wearing a gold chain around his neck and a gold bracelet on his wrist'.*

He said he felt embarrassed because he didn't have anything. She asked him for her parcel which he gave to her. They did not even stop for tea or coffee. They left straightaway and that was the last he saw of his once precious girlfriend for over thirty years.

He said he was devastated by what had happened and the contempt with which the love of his life had treated him. Professor Lynch added that he is still haunted by how they broke up and even *'though Monica and I are good friends now, it's still something that hurts me to this very day'.*

5

THE OXFORD DREAM

Professor Lynch said after his A' Levels in England, he applied to Oxford, Cambridge, and London Universities for a place to study Law. Oxford was his preferred choice as he used to walk around with his Oxford dictionary in Sierra Leone and felt some form of affinity with the College.

Johnathan Woods, who had coached him for his A' Levels also encouraged him to apply and he promised to provide him with a reference if he needed it.

When he discussed his plans with his landlord, Reverend Cole, however, he tried to dissuade him from applying to Oxford. He thought he would not stand a chance as a foreigner from Sierra Leone. He felt only rich English boys went to Oxford and Cambridge.

With his excellent A' Levels results, however, he was invited to an interview at Christ Church College, Oxford, for the faculty of Jurisprudence. The letter of invitation arrived on a Saturday in the presence of his landlord's sons and daughter. He said he jumped up and down in delight that he had been offered an interview.

The interview was attended by many potential students and their parents from other schools including Kings School Canterbury. He was the only black student at the interview, so he did not think he had a very good chance of being accepted.

Following the interview, Professor Lynch left Oxford and returned to Streatham. He said he told his landlord how the interview went and although he felt he had answered all their questions correctly, he was uncertain of his chances as the only black person there.

On a Saturday morning shortly after his interview, a letter came from Oxford and he said his hands trembled as he opened it. The letter said the university wanted to offer him a place. He jumped up and down with excitement and happiness again.

He did not have any money to pay his fees, so he called the secretary of Christ Church College in Oxford who told him his name was on the scholars' list.

Being on the list meant that following an interview, the College may provide a scholarship. She went to the dean and told him about the Professor's dilemma in taking up his place. He was given a scholarship on the basis of the strength of his A' Levels and the quality of his interview, which he gladly accepted.

As a scholar, it meant their gowns were different. They were identified by a longer undergraduate gown which was different from everyone else's.

The Professor said wearing this made him feel proud especially as he did not come from any of the famous schools like Eton or Harrow. He had got there through self-study and correspondence courses whilst working as a porter in a paint factory.

Professor Lynch told me he started Oxford University on 8th October 1965. He was twenty-one years old. When he started, he had no friends and he had difficulty with his subsistence because the scholarship did not cover all his needs.

There were many nice restaurants around such as the Michelle Bistro. He applied for a job there as a waiter and worked there in the evenings during term-time.

Unlike other universities which had twelve-week terms, Oxford University operated an eight-week term. This provided plenty of opportunity for private study and part-time work.

During the holidays, he returned to London and worked as a porter at the Royal Dental Hospital in Leicester Square. He said he used to make dental castes from Plaster of Paris so the students could use them to practise drilling and filling and so on.

He said he also did some work for a theatre costume designer called Morris Angel in Shaftesbury Avenue. He worked on the shop floor as a sales assistant to measure people and help with sales. The coat he wore two years later to dance with the Queen Mother was purchased from this shop.

Although he had only played football in Sierra Leone, he was taught how to play rugby at Oxford and became good at it. He joined the rugby team and became popular as a player for his college. He was fast on the wing and made many friends through rugby.

He said he graduated with a High 2nd Class Honours degree in 1968. He mentions two particular tutors, Mr Dingle Foot and Mr Quintin Hogg (Lord Hailsham) whom he credits with being helpful to him during this period.

6

THE SWITCH

Professor Lynch said his landlord was equally delighted at his success. He tried to get him a scholarship from Sierra Leone which would pay for him to do the Bar in England and then return home to be a practising barrister.

He came down from Oxford, back to Streatham, with a view to taking the Bar and qualifying to return home.

That was when the dilemma started.

He tried to get work with some law firms but none would hire him because they could not see him with their group of white lawyers. In those days, it was difficult to see a black lawyer in the firms.

Additionally, he was in trouble because his country would not help him with a scholarship to do the Bar.

Stuck in no man's land and his funds quickly running out, he decided to get a job. He went to work as a porter in St Bartholomew's Hospital, London. The pay was similar to what he used to earn as a porter at the Royal Dental Hospital but the work was lighter.

In the interview, the head porter was extremely surprised he wanted to work there. He asked why he wanted to be a porter when he had a degree from a great university. He told him that he was running out of money, could not get a job in a law firm, and neither could he return home.

Travelling to and from the hospital to work was tiring so he rented a one-bedroom accommodation in Smithfield from his scanty income.

He remembers sitting in the square one day, taking a short rest from doing errands at the hospital, when he saw some doctors walking across the square. He spotted one whose face looked familiar. He said he dashed up in excitement saying, *"Is that you David?"* He turned round and saw him and said, *"Oh my God, is that you Chris?"*

David was a medical student at the hospital and was on his way to do his teaching rounds. He was running late so he asked for his telephone number, which he wrote down and gave to him.

David Badenok used to play rugby with him in Oxford. Years later, he became the best man at Professor Lynch's wedding. Later that evening, David rang him up and asked why he was a porter at the hospital. He explained his dilemma to him.

David invited him for a drink at his hall of residence to catch up on rugby and other things. They went out and had a good meal and caught up on old times. David was the captain of the hospital rugby club, which was a strong side. It was made up of Oxford and Cambridge students who were doing their clinical training in London.

He invited the Professor to a match on the following Saturday, announcing he wanted him to play on his team. Professor Lynch said he was not sure it would be possible since he was not a medical student. David as team captain, reassured him it would not matter as he was a part of the hospital and they were one person short.

So, Professor Lynch played for them in what was a difficult match against St. Mary's Hospital in London in an inter-hospital competition. He said he played well and scored two tries in his first match against St. Mary's.

The President of the Rugby Club, Mr Edward Cope who was an ENT surgeon and also the Dean asked David who Professor was. David explained he knew Professor Lynch from Oxford University and that he had seen him working at the hospital as a porter and invited him to come and play for them.

The Professor said David later told him the Dean had been impressed by his rugby skills and had invited him to tea one day after work.

David took Professor Lynch to meet the Dean at his home office which was in Charter House Square and which also housed the student accommodation. They had tea with the Dean, his wife, and his son.

They talked for a long time and Professor told him about the difficulties he was facing. The Dean suggested to him that a few London Colleges offered places to non-medical graduates who wanted to pursue a career in medicine and had no science qualifications but already had a first degree, in order to encourage more people to enter the medical profession.

The idea appealed to Professor Lynch and after discussing it with his friend David, he decided to go ahead and apply as he had nothing to lose.

As a first year MB student with a degree in Arts, he said one of his teachers was Professor Sir John Roseblatt, the Nobel Prize winner for physics. The Professor said that later, as a Consultant Gynaecologist, he ended up carrying out a hysterectomy for Sir Roseblatt's wife..

It was a tough year because most of them had not done the sciences before. They had studied religion, arts, drama, and so on. It was quite a mixture of graduates and most had difficulty with the course.

The failure rate was seventy percent but those who were fortunate to pass the first year joined the science students in the second year. Professor Lynch was fortunate to have done well in the exam and proceeded to the second year, where he said they did Biochemistry, Physiology and Anatomy.

The Professor always talks about being the only black student in the second year which had one hundred and twenty students. When I asked him how that made him feel, he said, *'Walking into the room on the first day was intimidating. I felt insecure because there was no one else like me to relate to. So, it was a depressing experience. If there had been another black student or even a foreign student, perhaps I would have felt more comfortable.'*

He was grateful that he played rugby because his companions were his rugby teammates. That helped him to make friends and socialise and reduced the sense of isolation.

The Professor said his classmates and rugby mates were not always nice to him. There was some bullying going on as he was the only black student among them. He narrated a story to me about being in the locker room after a rugby match where he had scored the winning try.

Instead of congratulating him some of the guys decided to make fun of him and one said *'Christopher, where is your tail?'* However, without missing a beat he turned around and said *'It's right here in front of me.'* Then he added *'Everybody burst out laughing'.* Even as he narrated this story to me, he burst out laughing. It had obviously had the desired impact because he still found it funny.

He loved his rugby ball. He really wanted me to take a photograph of it. He kept asking me to take a photograph of the ball. For him, it has great significance. In consideration of the fact that it was a rugby ball which helped to get him noticed and into medical school, it is understandable. But I think it also reminded him of the days when he was younger, fitter and the toast of the team.

He still had no funding, so he continued to work as a porter. In his second year, the Dean of his medical school assisted him in getting a scholarship. That grant helped but he still had to meet his living expenses. He took on a second job at Smithfield Market as a porter, juggling two jobs to make ends meet whilst studying.

The second year was difficult for him and he often studied in the library until quite late. There were many times when he'd only leave as they were locking up. He said he was fortunate to pass with a good grade and was among the top five students in over a hundred and twenty.

He said the other students in his year were surprised that a black boy could be so clever even though they all knew he had come through with a good Honours degree from Oxford University.

He described an event to me as follows: *'A very funny thing happened in my college residence one day. I used to revise by using a tape recorder to record the lessons and then play it back to myself in my room. One day, I felt the need to go and visit the toilet but as I opened my door to go out of my room, three bodies came crashing into my room.*

My classmates wanted to know what trick I used to help me do so well in class, so they were outside my door eavesdropping. They were shocked to find out there was no one else in my room, only me and my tape recorder. I went to the toilet and came back, served them some coffee and then they returned to their rooms. That proved to them I did not have anyone helping me with my education. I was happy to have proved them wrong because I did not know what their intentions were'.

Professor Lynch did not talk about much of the abuse he endured but I know he experienced far more racially motivated abuse than just the two stories described so far.

During the year I worked with him it was a rarity for his children to accompany him to events or programmes, so I accompanied him to an alumni event in the Great Hall at St Bartholomew's Hospital (Barts) in London.

Many people who had studied with him and others whom he had worked with or mentioned to me during the process of writing this book were present. He was so happy to be among his peers and they seemed to enjoy seeing him and talking with him. He truly was in his element here- animated, challenged, and inspired. I had never seen him this way.

One of the Professor's past classmates sat between me and himself. On my other side sat another classmate and his wife. The gentleman sitting between myself and Professor Lynch told me they were really mean to him during their studies. He said there was a concert one day and they led the professor to the front of the room right in front of the stage.

Then the actors came out in black faces and were singing: *'Be careful about entering Room Number … (I've forgotten the number) you'd never know who would be in there'*. They said they were mocking him.

The man on my right recalled the song they were singing and they sang it together, sheepishly.

One of the men said to me *'His real name is Balo, Balgun, Ballo. He just likes to say Christopher'*. He was trying to pronounce *'Balogun'* but couldn't. And he was whispering this to me in earnest.

So, Professor Lynch went through a lot but he would never tell it if it would irritate or hurt anyone. His mantra is: *'My father used to say, 'walk softly among the tulips'*.

I would always say to him in response *'Sometimes you need to stamp on those tulips Professor'*. Maybe I shouldn't have said that because it turned out he is quite capable of stamping on the tulips especially if they are black women.

He did well in his second-year exams and progressed to the third year. By now, he had been in the country for more than five years. This made him eligible for a grant from the British Government which he applied for and received.

He was also now eligible for a British passport and so, in the same year, he received a British passport and was now a Black Briton. He said these helped make his third year a little bit easier.

He completed his studies with good grades and gained a Bachelor of Medicine and a Bachelor of Surgery (MBBS).

Professor Lynch was able to qualify for the Membership of the College of Surgeons (MRCS LRCP) final medical degree certificate a year before his final medical exams. This enabled him to secure locum appointments and begin work which helped him to improve the quality of his education even though he was yet to formally receive his degree. He said he was the only person who qualified with the gold medal in Pathology in the entire university.

The Professor became the Academic Affairs Officer for the University of London. He had strong political views in university: on Sundays he joined other students from the University of London, King's College, London School of Economics, and others to speak at Speakers' Corner in Hyde Park on political issues.

Years later when he reconnected with Monica she told him she'd heard he would usually go and speak at Speakers Corner. She thought he was just an idle bum and didn't realise he was a medical student, so she didn't want anything to do with him.

He represented London University (Barts was part of London University) in a number of debating meetings and was able to develop several new friendships.

During his time as the Academic Affairs Officer for students of the London University, he had a working relationship with Mrs Margaret Thatcher who was the Secretary of State for Education at that time and not yet Prime Minister.

His main job was to fight for academic support for the students and other academic matters such as tuition fees – a job he thinks he did successfully.

He was a student member of the Conservative Party, so he said they used to have heated debates and arguments with the other students especially those in the Labour Party. He contested the presidency of London University, which he did not win as a chap called Steven Creppal who was also a Conservative Party member won the election.

The National Student Union was made up of people like Jack Straw who later became Foreign Minister and others who became quite key in the UK's political life.

7

ALL WORK, AND NO PLAY

I said to Professor Lynch, *'what about your social life whilst you were studying, did you have any at all? It seems all you did was work and study. Talk to me about your social life'*.

And he said *'Yes It would be unjust if I did not dedicate a chapter to my social experience as a university undergraduate both in Oxford and London'*.

In Oxford, he befriended a female student in his faculty by the name of Lady Margaret Bennett. He described her as *'an intelligent girl, daughter of Lord Bennet of Comna in Oxfordshire'*. He said he was sure she befriended him because he was intelligent too and funny and she was 'enthusiastic' about him. Her father had been a colonial official and she had travelled with him when she was younger to various African countries.

She took Professor Lynch to her parents' home and introduced him to them. He said her parents showed him *'great kindness'* and took him into their home as a member of their family. Her father was a racehorse owner as well and took him to various race meetings.

They were part of high society and introduced him to their friends at race meetings and so on. He remembers that her father would always introduce him as the *'African boy from Sierra Leone'*. He was never introduced as Margaret's boyfriend.

I asked him how that made him feel especially as he said they made him a part of their family and he said *'this made me feel embarrassed but I didn't make a fuss about it'*. That was his mantra at work: *'Never trample on the tulips'*.

Lord Bennett had been a great rugby enthusiast and they attended many Oxford rugby matches together. He would also accompany Margaret to many of the Oxford dances and activities.

They graduated together but she decided to stay in Oxford and pursue her post-graduate studies in Law whilst he decided to move to London. They kept in touch and she carried on with her career in law and became a *'high-flyer'* in the field.

She got married to a fellow solicitor and they came to live in Highgate near Hampstead Heath. He was invited to her wedding to Mr Michael Simmonds.

It happened that when they had their first child, he had just become qualified as a doctor. He was a trainee senior house officer in obstetrics and gynaecology in his second post-graduate year. He was on duty when she came into labour and assisted with her delivery which was by caesarean section for protective reasons.

They kept in touch and Lady Bennett supported him in his post-graduate training and introduced him to many of her friends. He said he also helped her during the early days of motherhood. She invited him to the christening of her other children.

She unfortunately contracted breast cancer at the top of her profession and sadly died from it. He remained friends with her husband Michael, who continued his legal practice, though he has recently lost contact with him.

London University had four main halls of residence for students: The William Goodenough House, The Lillian Pencin Hall, The Connaught Hall, and the International Hall.

He said he managed to find himself a place in the International Hall, which housed international and English students from various faculties.

As he was one of the few medics in that hall, he made many friends and ran for the presidency of International Hall. He was duly elected and worked on student affairs and social events. He worked closely with the Master of Hall of Residence who was also a tutor in one of the colleges at the London University. He said they became good friends and worked well together.

As the president of the Hall, he ran various welfare and social committees. He supervised the social education committee which was run by another medic called Glin Tong. Glin was a medic from the Royal Free Hospital College.

I have been unable to locate a medic called Glin Tong and asked the Professor on several occasions if this was the correct spelling and each time, he has insisted that it is.

The International Hall was a famous hall of residence full of enthusiastic students. They would organise weekly dances on a Friday for intercollegiate interactions.

This was when he met his late friend, Mr Quashie Jones who was a successful businessman and ran a restaurant and bar called Toddies in Fulham Road, West London near Earl's Court.

It was a magnificent building on three floors. The top floor was the VIP area, the middle floor was for dinning, and the first floor was the area assigned to club activities and also had a bar. Mr Quashie Jones had been a chef in the army before he retired to set up his restaurant.

The basement was reserved for music and entertainment, where the artists of the time used to congregate and played everything from pop to jazz music. It was always packed and was frequented by well-known artists like Georgie Fame and Alan Price, Jimi Hendrix, Rod Stewart, Bob Marley and the Wailers, and other musicians from the Rolling Stones.

He said his friendship with Mr Quashie Forster Jones gave him the opportunity to meet these famous artists and mega personalities.

The Professor also said he met the late Princess Diana at Toddies as she used to go there with her friends. They would sit in the VIP lounge at the top for a night out or come in for a nightcap after a show.

The future wife of the Prince of Wales, Princess Diana was a teenager, about eighteen or nineteen years of age when he met her at Toddies.

Professor engaged some of the artists he met at *Toddies* to come and play at their social functions at the International Hall. One of them was the late artist Bob Marley who at the time, had a band called *Bob Marley and the Wailers.*

He said they had wonderful social events which he helped to organise and run. He remembers during his student days, he would spend many hours talking to Bob Marley and dancing to his music with the female students at his college.

A good number of Professor Lynch's student colleagues frequented these social activities on a Friday evening when they hired well-known bands to play music.

Also, annually they ran a graduation ball which meant famous artists would attend and perform contemporary music and provide great entertainment at the graduation ball once a year.

They also had evening sessions and conversations with Jimi Hendrix whose music they enjoyed listening to until the early hours of the morning. Sometimes, he and his friends would join Jimi Hendrix at his apartment in Bayswater with his Swedish girlfriend, drinking wine and other alcohol.

Professor Lynch said he was fortunate not to go off track with his education, even though the temptations were great and everywhere.

The company and entertainment were quite fascinating, but he said he kept steadfastly to his education.

Mr Quashie Foster Jones passed away in 2018 but the Professor had the opportunity of being in contact with his wife, Mrs Bernadette Foster Jones.

He was also involved with other social events such as debating with other colleges in the university.

At that time, Margaret Thatcher was Secretary of State for Education and as the University Academic Affairs Officer, he worked closely with her. He remembered she was a firm, stern minister interested in the welfare and education of students. They had several meetings where he put forward the case for student education and welfare quite firmly.

As an officer of the University Students Union, he would attend the annual university ball of London University. He had the opportunity to dance with the Queen Mother who was then the Chancellor of the University and only the Officers of the University could dance with her.

He said he was popular in the university. He had many girlfriends, both from Oxford and some he had met in London. They had great times together and enjoyed many social functions including the theatres.

A colleague of his told me he was popular with the ladies. He was handsome, charismatic, intelligent and full of life and the ladies *'just fell for him'*.

In the hall of residence, where he lived, there was a street in front of his building, on the other side of which was the nursing home of the Great Ormond Street Hospital.

At night, he and his friends used to communicate with the nurses in the home by torch light signs and they used those to send messages across, which he describes as *'very funny'*. Occasionally, if they had favourable responses, they would meet during the day to socialise.

At the lunch I attended at the Great Hall which I have described earlier his friend who described some of the abuse he encountered asked me: *'Did he tell you about the nurses across the street'*? I said *'Yes he did'*. He smiled and nodded as if to agree with what Professor had told me earlier that *'It was truly a wonderful experience'*.

There was a 'nice' square in front of their building called Bronvic Square. It was a special square with park benches and places to play limited sports. As students, they would gather in the square to play cards, interact, and socialise with colleagues. He said he enjoyed the social aspect of his student life and he would always remember the wonderful times he had at Barts and the International Hall in London.

He remembered when he was in Oxford, he also used to enjoy cricket and there he became friends with the current prime minister of Pakistan, the Honourable Imran Khan.

When Imran Khan lived in London after graduating from Oxford, Professor Lynch and his colleagues would visit his flat in Gloucester Road. When Imran became the captain of the Pakistan cricket team, they all went to Lords to witness his victory for Pakistan in the World Cup.

He was a 'nice' student colleague in politics and he said they socialised well and had some great times when he was in London. He hoped the Prime Minister would read his autobiography and remember the good times they had.

8

THE JOURNEY BEGINS

After graduation, getting a house job was mandatory as it was the introductory year to practising clinical medicine. It was an apprenticeship which involved six months of medicine and six months of surgery before they could continue with post-graduate education.

Professor said he was popular in the surgical department, probably because he was a good sportsman with high academic grades and a friendly personality.

He did his year of apprenticeship before his other colleagues in the university because he had qualified with the Membership of the College of Surgeons (MRCS LRCP) before his final university exams.

He did his first house job in Whipps Cross in medicine working for Doctor Winwood. He describes him as a good consultant specialist and general physician. He said Dr Winwood gave him a good start and foundation which helped him when he applied for his next job.

From there, he applied to be a house officer in general surgery at Barts Hospital where he'd started out as a porter, and which he was able to secure despite fierce competition.

He worked as Surgical House Officer to the Queen's Surgeon Sir Edward Tuckwell and Mr Martin Birnstingl. Everybody wanted that job because of the prestige of being associated with the Royal Family. Mr Tuckwell was the Sergeant Surgeon of Queen Elizabeth, the Queen Mother.

Sir Tuckwell was a keen sportsman himself and his sporting interest was cricket so they had something in common to talk about. He said Sir Tuckwell was keen for him to be appointed because of his university grades and because his favourite cricketer at the time was the captain of the West Indies, someone called Clive Lloyd. There were even times he would forget Professor Lynch's name and call him Clive. He offered him the House Officer's post during the interview.

Owing to the sensitive and high-profile nature of the job, the interview process was rigorous. They had to pass with the consultant before being given the job. Just after his interview, Mr Tuckwell was invited to Canada to examine for the post-graduate Fellowship as a visiting surgeon.

In the meantime, the job of the house officer in surgery, which had already been offered to him, was advertised and a meeting had taken place where the house officer position was allocated to another doctor in his year called Tom Morgan and another fellow whose name he could not recall.

The Professor was left out in the cold even though he was one of the best candidates, and Mr Tuckwell for whom, he would be working had already offered him the job during the interview.

A list had been put out which excluded him. He said he thought to himself that this must be a racially motivated decision. Professor Lynch said this was his first experience of racism at work. When I asked him how it made him feel he said *'I felt dejected, depressed and I thought there was no hope'*.

When Sir Edward Tuckwell returned from his visit to Canada, the Professor made an appointment to see him and told him what had happened. Sir Edward was furious because he knew he was the right candidate to work for him and he called for a meeting with his colleagues.

He told them he did not know what had happened but Professor Lynch was the best medical student and he had already promised him the position as his House Officer. There was a heated argument but they came to an amicable compromise: Tom and the Professor were appointed and the third candidate was given the opportunity to come at the next rotation after six months.

So, he worked as a house officer to Sir Edward Tuckwell, the Queen Mother's Surgeon. He would take him to the surgery of his private patients in his practice at the King Edward VII Hospital where he treated royals. He introduced Professor Lynch to the Queen Mother with whom he became well acquainted.

As house officers to Sir Edward Tuckwell, the Queen Mother's Surgeon, the Professor and Tom wore a rose on their robe to differentiate them from the other doctors. He said each morning when they went to work there was a fresh rose to wear. The rose became a trademark of the way Professor dressed later on. He was never fully dressed without a rose stuck neatly to his jacket.

The Professor had already met the Queen Mother as a student when she was the Chancellor of London University and he was the Academic Affairs Officer of the Students' Union. He had had his first dance with the Queen Mother during his final year, not knowing he would be privileged to dance with her again later on in his career.

I wanted to know more about his first dance with the Queen Mother and so I probed him to find out how she reacted to him. He said, *'I remember during that first dance, she was shy but pleasant. She did not ask me any questions, probably, because she did not want to ask the wrong ones and perhaps offend me. She was a good dancer but, of course, I was also a good dancer as I had been a keen student of Sylvester, (Sylvester was the ballroom dancer whose book he used to study when he was in school in Sierra Leone) and I loved ballroom dancing.'*

Now, as the house officer to Sir Edward Tuckwell, he met her again professionally and also on several occasions when he was invited by Mr Tuckwell to special royal functions.

Professor Lynch described working for Mr Tuckwell, the Queen Mother's Surgeon, as an immense pleasure. He had little or no complications as far as his patients were concerned. He was fast but careful. He always wanted to make sure his House Officers were happy and given priority of any surgical discipline they wanted to improve on in the department. He was a good teacher and an exemplary person.

He was good to everyone and also trustworthy, a man who led the department with compassion and skill. When he saw a porter, he would ask if he was doing alright, that was the type of man Mr Tuckwell was.

That statement about the porter reminded me of an incident with Professor Lynch recently. At the hospital where he was receiving treatment, a middle aged Filipino nurse was really excited to see him. She fussed over him even though he did not recognise her. She said, *"you do not remember me but I remember you. I was a cleaner when you used to work here as a Senior Consultant. You would always stop to say hello to me."* Looking at what he said about Mr Tuckwell, I think he took on more than just professional training from a man he seems to hold in high esteem.

Being the good teacher Mr Tuckwell was, he put things in simple terms for everyone to understand and he made difficult theories look simple.

Mr Tuckwell would have a special meeting with his house men to look at the prepared operating list and ask them which surgery they would like to do under his supervision. The operations were done on Thursdays because it gave him time to see the patient on the Friday before he returned to his country home in Petersfield, Surrey for the weekend.

On Wednesday afternoons, it was usually sports activities for the medical students. They did rugby training in Hyde Park and Mr Tuckwell used to go for walks with his wife in Hyde Park by the Serpentine River around the same time when they were training. Sometimes, they would stop and watch them training.

His London home was close to Hyde Park, whilst he consulted in Harley Street where he had his private practice.

Occasionally, Mr Tuckwell would invite them across to his London house for tea with his wife whom Professor described 'as kind and keen to support her husband's trainee doctors climb up the professional ladder'.

Mr Tuckwell was his first experience of an exceptionally successful surgeon. The professor remembers: 'he used to do a gall bladder operation in about eight minutes, skin to skin,' (start to finish).

Similarly, with his high-profiled private patients where he was a leading surgeon, he would take them along with his senior registrar to help him with the surgery. Professor Lynch said he enjoyed this very much indeed especially when they visited the Queen Mother.

He describes his entire experience of working for Mr Tuckwell as exemplary, because he said 'Mr Tuckwell taught me how to deal with patients' anxiety and that they should always be the priority. He taught me that I must never let my patients down and I must always recognise that my patients were depending on me because they have no one else to rely on for help'.

The Professor concluded his introductory experience to postgraduate surgery after six months which he said was made 'memorable' by Sir Edward Tuckwell.

The Professor's next move was to decide on what he wanted to do as a postgraduate doctor. He was torn between the medical training of Dr Winwood with whom he had worked in his first job whilst doing his training in medicine, and that of his recent one as a trainee surgeon under Mr Tuckwell.

He decided to follow the line between medicine and surgery — Obstetrics and Gynaecology. Obstetrics had a lot of medical input, whilst Gynaecology had a lot of surgical input so he felt he was the winner either way.

After completing his apprenticeships in medicine and surgery in 1975, he applied for further training as an anatomy demonstrator at Barts Hospital in order to gain a better understanding of surgery.

He said Professor O.J. Lewis who was the Professor of Anatomy remembered him from when he was a student and apparently had a high regard for his talent and performance. There were a number of other applicants for the job but he was one of the lucky candidates appointed.

In January 1976, he joined the department as an anatomy teaching staff member responsible for teaching medical students. He taught the principles of anatomy whilst training for his first exam in the Fellowship of Surgery.

Professor said he took good care of his students and they were happy with his training. He did not realize the positive feedback from them went back to Professor Lewis, who was from New Zealand.

He was pleased with his work and Professor was content with the attention he received in the classroom. He said his students even gave him an award called, *'Anatomy Demonstrator Extraordinaire'*.

In the summer of that year, he took a holiday to France. Coincidentally, the Barts Hospital Rugby Club, of which he was a member, had also organised a tour to Paris to play rugby.

He met someone at one of the rugby matches who had been at Barts with him. His name was Andrew Peacock. Andrew told Professor Lynch he was working in one of the hospitals in Paris. The Professor was curious to know more so Andrew invited him to his hostel at the hospital.

He showed Professor Lynch around the hospital and what he did working as a Registrar in an American Hospital in Paris. He was enjoying practising medicine in the intensive care unit and the patients were nice. Andrew said that even though he was fed hospital food, it was a pleasant place.

The Professor asked him how he got the job and he told him he had been appointed through an open competition, even though he had trained in England. Andrew offered to introduce him to his trainer, Professor Thomas Hughes. They met with Professor Hughes at the hospital and the rest is history.

At the lunch in the Great Hall at Barts, I met Andrew Peacock. He was so excited to see Professor Lynch again. He had brought with him a photograph of their batch at Barts and showed me and the professor the photograph.

They reminisced about old times and they both tried to narrate the same story to me as the professor had already done before. It felt like déjà vu to me. It was as though people were literally stepping out of the pages of a book and coming to life.

Dr Thomas Hughes, who was from the USA told Professor Lynch he could work in their hospital in Paris whenever he wanted to in general surgery training and his trainer would be Mr Lalong.

He was excited by the possibility of working in France as a Registrar in intensive care. He replaced Andrew Peacock who left the following year to return to England to continue his training in medicine.

He said he was a bit apprehensive at first because his French was not very good as he had only done O' Level French at school. In any case, they were provided with a French teacher at the hospital and they always had a nurse to help them with the interpretation. Interestingly, he admitted he learnt most of his French in the nightclubs they frequented at weekends.

He said the work was pleasant and he dealt with emergency admissions, intensive care patients, monitoring patients who had received surgery by the consultants and those with medical problems who were under the care of physicians.

He worked with an American and a Canadian doctor. The three of them worked as colleagues on a rotation - ten days on and ten days off. This gave him the opportunity to go to Germany, and Italy, and see more of France.

On one of his ten days off, he drove his car to Stuttgart in Germany to visit the Mercedes Benz plant and see how they manufactured cars. When he arrived in front of the Mercedes Benz plant, his car stalled and broke down. He had it looked at by the engineers there but because it was an old car- a Mercedes 280 SL hard top- he was told the engine had perished beyond repair.

So there and then, he recalled asking them what it would cost to get a new engine. The price, though high, was just within his reach. As he had to get back to Paris, he asked them to replace his old engine with a new one. So, he got a brand-new engine directly from the Mercedes Benz plant.

This anecdotal story he narrates to me with fondness and amazement - that his old car chose to die right in front of the Mercedes Benz factory thus providing him with the right engine for the car.

By looking after their patients for ten consecutive days, he said they got to know their patients well and vice versa which was mutually beneficial.

9

THE GREAT AND THE GOOD

On one Saturday in Autumn, he was sitting with his colleagues in the casualty room watching a rugby match being played between England and France on TV. They were glued to the *'box'* when an almighty sound came from the emergency department.

The ambulance siren broke through the noise and news came that someone had suffered a cardiac arrest. They got up and waited for the patient to arrive.

The Professor and his fellow doctors were informed it was a head of state who had been visiting his embassy. He was with his country's ambassador when he went into cardiac arrest after lunch.

He said he was all geared up and he called his Consultant who was on duty with him to let him know and within minutes the Consultant was there. As Professor started performing cardiac massage and resuscitation, he realised this was an African gentleman.

They ripped off his clothing and he started massaging his chest. He shocked him with two hundred joules of electric current five times to get his heart beating but it failed to resuscitate him. His Consultant who was French, told him the man was dead, (Il est mort) but the Professor was single-minded and decided to try again for the sixth time. Then he noticed there was cardiac activity.

They quickly gave him some medicine via a drip to stabilize his heart's rhythm and strength because it was beating fast. Professor had broken about six of the patient's ribs in the process. They quickly took him to the intensive care department and connected him to the cardiac monitor.

As Professor Lynch read the patient's notes, he realized he was the president of his home country, Sierra Leone, President Siaka Probyn

Stevens. He was shocked to see that he had performed resuscitation on the President of his country.

He was in intensive care for six days recovering slowly. His ribs were displaced but he did not need surgery.

During his time in hospital, he asked the ICU nurse who Professor Lynch was. She told him he was a doctor from England. He asked what country he had come from originally but she did not know. The ICU nurse then asked Professor Lynch which country he had originally come from and he told her he was from Sierra Leone.

President Stevens was both shocked and pleased. He was now even more keen to speak to Professor Lynch.

When Professor Lynch went to speak with him, he asked him if he knew who he was. Professor confirmed he did but that as a doctor it was not his place to focus on his or anyone else's status and that he had thought it right not to disturb him given the pain he was in. Professor Lynch told him that he was, however, pleased to have been able to save his life.

President Stevens did recover completely and with the consent of the Professor's Consultant, he discharged him. Professor Lynch said he was congratulated for doing a good job and became highly regarded by the President.

Life is interesting in the way it leads you to be exactly where you must be at the right time and for the right purpose. Here was Professor Lynch saving the life of the President of the country he had wanted to return to in order to practice law. The country had not responded when he called, but if she had, then he would not have become a medical doctor and saved the President's life that day.

When President Siaka Stevens was discharged, he moved to an affluent part of Paris. A few weeks after his discharge, Professor Lynch received a letter inviting him to dinner.

He took with him the nurse who helped him with his care. He said her name was Maria and he thought she was pretty. They had a pleasant time and a very good dinner which impressed nurse Maria and he hoped, increased his chances of being with her.

I remember hearing this part of his story and wondering why a visit to a President was required to increase one's chances with someone you wanted to date. Surely being a nurse who worked with you, she would know the kind of man you were and therefore be able to decide if she liked you. I did not quite understand his need to work so hard to impress her. But hey, those were just my thoughts. I was not there to understand the circumstances or dynamics of the relationship.

They enjoyed the wine and he found President Stevens to be a nice man despite all the negative publicity about him. I asked him what kind of negative things people said about the President. He said people had said he was a tribalist but in any case, he had come into the hospital dying so he really did not have a choice of who treated him.

The Professor and Maria returned to the hospital after a night full of jokes and laughter and they started dating after this.

Siaka Stevens had a good friend who attended his recovery; the late Fidel Castro with whom he was friends for many years. The Professor had the pleasure of meeting him at Siaka Stevens' mansion in Avenue Foch in Central Paris.

He said he was privileged to meet this great man he had heard and read so much about. He was a humorous individual and Siaka Stevens told him he was one of the best brains in the world.

He said Fidel Castro said to him, *"Doctor, you are in a noble profession, but in my profession as President of Cuba, there are three things I need to do to keep my people happy:*

One, I have to give them good health.

Two, I need to give them good education, and

Three, I have to keep them happy.

Without these three, I cannot succeed as a president. If they have good health, they can go and work and pay taxes. If they have good education, they can make good judgements and assess propositions put to them, and the third would give them the chance to decide right from wrong".

Professor Lynch said he thought those were wise comments, but he was happy he was a physician and not a politician. He felt President Castro was a man of good company and enterprising ideas.

Later in 1988, Siaka Stevens died and one of his successors, President Ahmed Tejan Kabba, (who governed the country from 1996 - 2007) invited Professor Lynch to receive the Medal of Honour of the Republic of Sierra Leone in Freetown. Professor said he was sad President Siaka Stevens had died but he was ecstatic about the invitation and felt highly honoured.

He continued working in the hospital treating many distinguished patients because it was a well-known and respected hospital in Paris. It had doctors from many parts of the world and the quality of care provided by those doctors was high.

According to Professor Lynch, the hospital was recognised as part of the United States in 1913 and was famous for treating key world figures.

He said he was very lucky to be a member of the team and he met ambassadors, actresses and actors. He said he even treated Mrs Simpson who was the wife of the abdicated King of England - Edward VIII who lived on the same street as the hospital in the western suburbs of Paris.

One of his patients at the hospital was called Monsieur Goudeket. He was the husband of the late Marie Colette, a famous French writer and the head of the French evening newspaper called France Soir.

He came in as a patient with Tuberculosis and fluid in his lungs. He did not know he had TB until Professor Lynch examined him and discovered he had a lung infection. So, he drained the fluid from his chest and sent it off for analysis which showed the diagnosis was tuberculosis.

Draining the fluid from his lungs gave him comfort with his breathing before they started his treatment. He was treated effectively and recovered quite well and was discharged from hospital.

His partner at the time, Madam Gyling, owned a well-known perfumery called Gyling. They were a pleasant couple. On his discharge, he invited the Professor to their flat in San Tropez and said anytime he was down in the South of France he should pop in.

Monsieur Goudeket wrote a book a few years later with the title 'The delights of growing old'. Professor said he was delighted when Monsieur Goudeket signed his copy with the words 'To Monsieur Lynch, to whom I owe the delights of growing old'. The Professor said the book meant a lot to him. He still has it and showed it to me with Monsieur Goudeket's words.

Professor played rugby for a team in Paris called *Boi de Bolougue*. He also had an additional temporary teaching assignment, even though his French was not too good. The teaching assignment in medicine was at the Mont Mart which is a university in Paris.

He was invited to teach by the Dean of the university who had been to the hospital as a patient and was impressed with the care he received from Professor. He asked if he would join his faculty, which Professor agreed to do. He said he made many friends and had a wonderful experience.

One day, he was on duty following a nice short vacation. A patient came to casualty, not with a heart attack this time but chest pain. Professor Lynch admitted him to the intensive care unit, put a chest monitor on him to record his heart rate which had dropped beats but he had very little symptoms of shortage of breath.

With his experience from the UK and having worked with Dr Winwood, the cardiologist during his training, he diagnosed that he had a heart block. His Consultant asked him if he had seen or ever put in a pacemaker before. He told him he had put in pacemakers when he was working with Dr Winwood in the UK.

His Consultant said he could put in a pacemaker which he did and within a short time the heart rhythm was corrected. The man lived in Fontainbleau, just south of Paris. He owned a vineyard which made very good wines. They had a good chat after his surgery as he was in hospital for a long time.

Before going home, he asked the Professor what he could do for him to show his appreciation. He told him his services were not for reward as he was paid by the hospital and he treated everyone according to their needs with the same degree of sympathy and respect.

This was a trait, he said he learnt from Sir Edward Tuckwell, who had told them *'your kindness and compassion for your patients should be without any wish for reward, you'll enjoy medicine better that way'*.

So, he told the French vineyard owner he was not interested in any fees for his service and was just happy to see him well. The patient insisted he would like to do something for him.

The year was 1976 and it was a very hot summer in Europe. Monsieur RayLand said the grapes that year were of extremely good quality and when he harvested it for his wine, he would like to name the red wine 'Lynch' after him - *'The Grapes of Lynch'*.

To the Professor's surprise, that same year, he was in his residence in the hospital when a van delivered to him twelve bottles of this very nice wine called Chateau Lynch. He said he still purchases it from time to time from wine merchants in the UK but it's very expensive and he cannot afford to have it very often.

I confirm I have not only seen the wine but tasted it. It is of the best quality- delicious, sweet and fruity.

The Professor said the wine was pleasant and he and Marie enjoyed it together. He gave a bottle to his Consultant, Thomas Hughes, and told him the story. Doctor Hughes loved the wine and made contact with the vineyard for regular delivery and supplies.

Professor Lynch loved his experience of living and working in Paris; treating all these famous people, having a wonderful experience with his work and getting appreciations from patients from all walks of life.

He was sad when it was time to leave Paris but managed to extend his contract there by two months. His next job was working for Professor Sir Alexander Turnbull in Oxford as a Senior House Officer/Junior Registrar.

10

HOME IS WHERE THE HEART IS

In 1978 when Professor Lynch got back to England, he drove straight to Oxford to sort out his accommodation and other logistics. He said he was going to miss Paris, having experienced a good life and peace and happiness there.

Unfortunately, things did not progress with Maria the nurse because her parents did not want her to leave France and her nursing profession. So, they remained friends by correspondence and saw each other on the occasional holiday visits.

He said it was a situation which made them both sad because things were looking bright for them. It was his second serious relationship and he said he felt they would have got married, if they had been able to keep the relationship together.

England and France are not a continent away and there are many hospitals in the UK where Maria could have carried on her nursing career. Professor might have been upset their relationship had ended but she had chosen to do so. These minor obstacles do not stand in the way of true love.

When he arrived in Oxford, he was welcomed for the third phase of his post-graduate training under the supervision and direction of Professor Sir Alexander Turnbull who was the Nuffield Professor and Head of Obstetrics and Gynaecology in Oxford.

The Professor said he was appointed senior house officer/junior registrar in gynaecology. His senior registrar was a Scottish doctor called Ian McKenzie to whom he was assigned and he supervised all his work in partnership with Sir Alex Turnbull.

Professor Lynch said he was kind to him and taught him a lot. He said he had heard recently, that he had suffered a stroke which was sad.

His job included being the principal contact for all patient care working in partnership with a colleague called Kevin Dalton who trained in London and is now a Professor in Cambridge - Rosie Maternity Hospital. They got on well together, shared duties and had mutual respect and helped each other; forming a good team.

Everything went well and Sir Alex was a great teacher for maternal care with a worldwide reputation. He was mainly an obstetrician rather than a gynaecologist. He also taught research methods and presentation.

Conversely, Professor also received surgical training from Mr Douglas Ellis, who was the second Consultant in the hospital and he was mainly a surgeon and gynaecologist. Thus, he said he was fully equipped for career progression receiving obstetrics training from Sir Alex and gynaecology and surgical exposure from Dr Ellis.

He said Kevin Dalton was a nice chap and they worked together well. Their flats were on the same corridor so they usually compared notes, helped each other with difficult tasks and if Kevin had to go off early, Professor Lynch would cover for him.

The Professor hardly went off early because he had no family to go to in Oxford. He shared his experiences in Paris with Kevin including details of his girlfriend, Maria. He said they used to chat about her day and night as he was unhappy to be separated from her.

Professor introduced Kevin to one of his French dishes called *Poulet Fume*. This was smoked chicken which he had learned to cook when he was working in L'Hopital American in Paris.

During some of his spare time in Paris, Professor Lynch would go round the kitchen and make friends with the staff and the chefs and they taught him how to make *Poulet Fume* and other French dishes.

He would cook it in his flat in Oxford and the other doctors would come and enjoy it. They knew Professor Lynch had worked in France and learnt to cook this special dish and, of course, he knew the nice wines so he chose the ones they would drink and they thoroughly enjoyed themselves.

Professor Lynch moved from the flat to a little house in Oxford, sharing the house with a Jewish post-graduate paediatrician called Ruby Shalon. She lived on the top floor whilst he lived on the ground floor. He was able to do more cooking because it had a bigger kitchen and his colleagues would come over for dinners and parties.

Sir Alex Turnbull asked him about his career so he told him where he was from. He told him he would be very valuable to his country if he decided to go back and work there whilst he still did a portion of his career in the UK. Sir Alex said he would support him at all times and he would write some fine references for him if he ever needed them.

I do wish I had asked the Professor why he had not taken up Sir Turnbull's suggestion to help his home country, Sierra Leone. Professor often lamented about poverty and corruption in Africa and it might be this is what put him off. Or maybe he was just focused on progressing his career at the time. I can only guess.

The Professor said he came to know Sir Alex's family very well. He knew his daughter and he was like a son in the family, apart from being his trainee at the hospital.

One day, Professor Sir Alex Turnbull visited Professor Lynch at his new house primarily to help him with the paper he was writing on appendicitis. He wanted to look it over and show him how to write publications for the journal.

To his surprise, he saw the photograph of Professor dancing with the Queen Mother at the university ball. He was extremely shocked that he could be in a position to dance with the Queen Mother.

They talked about the good old days when he was acting as a politician and studying medicine and his interactions with some important people he had met including the late Margaret Thatcher. The Professor said Sir Alex was impressed and his attitude changed towards him from that day.

I am not sure what that statement meant. The Professor had already said Sir Alex treated him well. Maybe there was a reduction in that silent patronisation which some English people give to their former colonials no matter how accomplished they are.

11

TRY SOME HAGGIS

Professor Lynch put himself forward for membership to the Royal College of Obstetrics and Gynaecology which was a part of the required training in Gynaecology. That was the final part of the training he needed to move on.

Sir Alex Turnbull helped him a lot with his studies and he passed the exam at the first attempt. Sir Alex Turnbull was delighted when he came back and gave him the good news and he said he never had any doubts about his ability and praised him for the progress he was making in his training.

The Professor now needed to look for a registrar's job in surgical training so he started looking at the journals for advertisements in surgery. He saw an advert for surgical training as a registrar in general surgery under Professor Sir James Fraser who was the President of the College of Surgeons of Edinburgh, Scotland.

He applied, and was fortunately appointed to his Department of Surgery though this was not based in Scotland but in England at the Royal Southampton Hospital.

He said he worked well with the team and Professor Sir James Fraser taught him a lot of skilful surgical techniques at a more advanced level. He always walked into the theatre with a limp but he was of immense calibre as a surgeon and he gave him lots of experience in general surgery.

Sir James Fraser could see his skill and his theoretical knowledge and that year he was able to take the final part of the Fellowship of General Surgery in Edinburgh.

Sir James Fraser recommended he take the exam in Edinburgh because he was from Edinburgh himself and of course the choice was obvious but it was also true that the training in Edinburgh was excellent.

Professor Lynch had taken the first part of the exam in England and now planned to take the final part of the fellowship exam in Edinburgh.

He booked a hotel in King Street in Edinburgh near the college. Having come from Southampton to spend the night in London, he then took the train from London to Edinburgh the following morning.

He arrived at his hotel in Edinburgh and did his last-minute revision preparing for his exam on Monday. He said he revised his work in his hotel so loudly he must have offended his next-door neighbours although they did not complain.

On the Monday, he went to do the theoretical part of the exam which was in two parts. The first paper was the principles of surgery and the second was on operative surgery.

He found the papers difficult but fortunately he had already had practical training which helped him. He did not feel confident at all in that final examination in general surgery in Edinburgh.

The following day all of those who had taken the exam returned to the Royal College of Surgeons of Edinburgh for the results. They were all standing around, in a large hall, some walking up and down, all of them waiting nervously to hear the results.

The examination secretary came onto the stage in the college to announce the results and he remembered his examination number was ninety-nine.

As she read out all the numbers, they listened and hugged whoever's name had been called. When she called out his number as having passed the exam, he said he leapt up in the air and fell on the floor because he was so overwhelmed with joy that he had passed.

She called out another four numbers before she said, *"ladies and gentlemen that's all. Thank you for coming"*. They found out only thirty-one candidates had passed out of the three hundred who had taken the exam.

The examination results were disappointing for the college but Sir James was happy because he had passed and had passed well. He had called him as soon as he received the news.

He said he was so overwhelmed by his results he decided to leave Edinburgh that very night to get back, stopping first in London before going back to Southampton. He was also quite hungry as he had not eaten all day worrying about the exam results.

When he arrived at the train station in Edinburgh, he saw food being sold in the shape of parcels and they looked interesting. He later learnt they were called *'Haggis'*.

They were apparently some kind of minced meat made into a parcel covered by pigs' bladder. He asked the Scottish woman selling it and she said it was one of the best Scottish dinners he would ever have and he should try it.

Not knowing what it was he asked her how to cook it. She told him all he had to do was put it in a saucepan with water, cover it up and let it boil. She mentioned some people don't bother to cover the pan because once it starts to boil the heat would cook it.

He bought some and took it to his flat in London where he was staying for a few days before going back to Southampton. He put it on the boil and went to the toilet to urinate. To his surprise, when he came out of the toilet the parcel had burst, the water in the pan was still boiling and most of the meat was on the floor.

He said he was disappointed but he scraped some of the meat back into his pan. He was too hungry to care and he was still emotionally exhausted from waiting for news of his results that morning. That was the sad ending of what had been a glorious day. In spite of this, he said he enjoyed his first introduction to Haggis.

When he arrived back at work, Professor Sir James Fraser greeted him with a lot of joy and gave him a hug. Professor Lynch said he felt like his son. Sir James Fraser organised a dinner party for him at his house with his wife and his two sons who were also medical students at that time.

His contract as a Registrar in general surgery with his Fellowship had now been completed with tremendous surgical training from good and outstanding senior colleagues.

Towards the end of the contract, he had started looking for a new job and had applied as a registrar in gynaecology to follow on the trail of his training.

He was offered an interview but the appointment committee was meeting on the same day he was taking his final fellowship exam in Edinburgh, so unfortunately, he could not attend the interview.

He wrote a polite letter to inform the appointment team he could not attend the interview because he was taking his final surgical fellowship examination in Edinburgh.

They were sympathetic and said they would consider his application but not at the expense of any other worthwhile candidates.

He said he did not regret missing the interview as he had now got the Fellowship in Surgery which would help him get other appointments.

To his surprise he received a letter from the Head of Gynaecology,

Mr Gordon Bourne at St Bartholomew's Hospital saying he had been appointed in absentia as a Registrar in the Department.

The letter stated he would also like to wish him well in the final surgical fellowship exam in Edinburgh. Professor Lynch said he did not bother to write back but instead he phoned Mr Bourne's secretary.

He was in theatre at the time, operating, and he gave her the message to pass onto Mr Bourne to let him know he was grateful for the appointment in absentia and he had been fortunate to have passed the final surgical examination in Edinburgh.

When Mr Bourne received the message, he called him back before going into his next operation. He congratulated him on passing and told him he was the one who had insisted he be considered in absentia and he was so pleased he did not let him down and had passed the exam.

He welcomed Professor Lynch to the department as a registrar in gynaecology and said he would want him to work for him. The Professor was pleased because Mr Bourne was the Head of the Department and the Senior Consultant.

Leaving his surgical course in Southampton as a fully trained surgeon, he was now embarking on the final leg of training as an obstetrician/gynaecologist at St Bartholomew's Hospital in London.

He said he felt thankful for all the training experience he had received in particular with Sir James Fraser who was his mentor. He felt confident taking up the position of surgical registrar in obstetrics and gynaecology at Barts.

Mr Bourne who was the head of the department was pleased to have him working for him because he could be relieved of some of his surgical commitments. He would entrust him with some of his private patients when he went away on holiday.

At that time, the consultants could go on holiday provided they had reliable and competent junior staff to cover for them. Mr Bourne would go away on a lecture tour to Iran or Jordan and leave Professor Lynch as his Registrar in charge of all his patients, both NHS and private. On weekends, when Mr Bourne was not there, he said he coped *'elegantly and confidently.'*

Professor Lynch describes Mr Bourne as an extremely good surgeon with good results and a good name who operated on many rich and famous women. He was a generous man. He offered Professor Lynch money from the proceeds of his private patients whom the Professor had been looking after. Professor told him it was not possible for him to accept the gift as he was his trainee and had a duty to assist him at all times including the times when he was absent. He said he told him, *'my dear son, don't argue with me just accept it and we'll talk'.* Professor did so, reluctantly.

The Professor had now come full circle. This is the hospital where he worked as a porter, unsure of what the future held. It was here he had received his first opportunity to study medicine. He was now returning as a Registrar. The wonders of life's rhythms.

12

CHOSEN

The final stage of his training to become a Consultant Obstetrician/Gynaecologist included a four-year appointment as a Senior Registrar. This appointment enabled candidates to refresh their clinical experience and education.

More particularly to receive training on the specialist subjects of their choice and other areas such as management, interpersonal relationships, and financial management of their departments.

Becoming a consultant involved an enormous responsibility for the education and training of future doctors. Teaching, training, research, and how to run a department are all important.

The budget of the department would not only become your responsibility but will enable you to compete with other budgetary departments.

This appointment was for four years, enabling the trainee to master all these aspects of final training. Fortunately for Professor Lynch, he had gone through a serious and comprehensive post-graduate training passing all the examinations at first attempt.

He had developed good interpersonal relationships with his trainers and members of staff. He said he felt confident he would do a good job as a consultant.

He said he still had at the back of his mind the fact that he was black and to get a good job, he had to be conscious about this because there had been a lot of insider communications and dealings which might affect his appointment.

I asked him what he meant by insider dealings and communications, and he said people call each other and have conversations and make decisions which one is unaware of. The situation depended greatly on who you knew and he did not know anyone of influence except the people he worked with.

Sir Marcus Setchell, the Queen's Gynaecologist, was also a member of staff at Barts. The appointment was for four years sequentially; two years to be spent at Barts, then two years at a peripheral hospital, Hackney Hommerton and The Mothers'.

Two registrars were to be appointed as Senior Registrars. One was to spend the first two years at Barts whilst the other would spend the first two years at Hackney Hommerton and The Mothers' Hospital. But they had the opportunity to attend special sessions at Barts to continue training.

One of the purposes of the appointment was academic. It was working for the Professor of Obstetrics and Gynaecology who at that time was Professor Timothy Chard, a well-respected and able doctor.

The other post was to work for the Queen's Gynaecologist and Head of Department, Sir Marcus Setchell at Barts. All the applicants wanted to work for the Queen's Gynaecologist.

The Professor said he saw the advert in the British Medical Journal inviting candidates to apply for the post of Senior Registrar, Chief Assistant to the Department of Obstetrics and Gynaecology at Barts Hospital.

The job description was clear and comprehensive. The appropriate entry qualifications were listed and the demands of the job were outlined.

When discussing his chance of getting one of the jobs with Mr Gordon Bourne, he did not talk him out of the application but he made it clear that there would be many other good candidates from other hospitals who would be applying. Unbeknown to Professor Lynch, Mr Bourne already had someone else in mind for the job.

The first thing Professor Lynch did was to go to the admissions medical staffing office to get a copy of the appropriate job description, which the secretary of appointments gave to him.

He photocopied it so he could study it in his flat in Charter House Square just outside the hospital. It was quite an elaborate document. So, he spent the weekend going through it and underlining salient aspects.

Having secured the particular job he was applying for, he went and discussed the prospects of his appointment with the Consultants-Shepherd, Bourne, Setchell, Evans and others. No one could guarantee him the job because it was a highly competitive job and the best candidate would be appointed.

He felt a bit disappointed after doing his research because he did not think he stood a good chance. He still did not give up, however, because he knew his training so far had been quite good.

On the day of the interview, to give a good impression he was smartly dressed in a three-piece suit with a gold chain in his waistcoat which he was given by one of the ladies whose husband he had treated.

There were seven consultants at the interview, one of them he recognised as Professor Reginald Shooter. He was a Consultant Pathologist for the hospital and had travelled extensively in Africa and Asia during his own training.

In Professor Lynch's medical school days, they used to have chats about malaria and other diseases he encountered when he was training as a postgraduate student in Africa.

Professor Shooter used to play squash with his consultant colleagues and Professor Lynch served them ginger beer in the bar as a medical student. He recognised he was one of the candidates applying for the post, although it did not make any difference whatsoever because there were six other consultants on the panel.

He was the Chairman of the interview panel. The others were a mixture of physicians, gynaecologists, and obstetricians.

He was the first to be interviewed because of his name, B Lynch. He said he was nervous and timid without much degree of confidence. Sweating and wiping his forehead with his handkerchief. He said he no doubt looked quite confused, but the panel were very kind and asked him to take a few moments and settle down.

The first question he was asked was how he felt about his training experience at Barts. He said he had his training quite categorically listed and he was happy with all the training. He spoke highly of his consultants who trained him and the opportunity he had had in understanding the care of patients; how to allay their fears, and how to be a good doctor.

There were six other candidates interviewed after him. There were two ladies and four men from different hospitals in the country coming to Barts for the post of Senior Registrar and Chief Assistant to the Queen's Gynaecologist. He said 'You can well imagine the high calibre of those candidates who attended'.

The interview was so elaborate it had to be split into two sessions: four, including himself, were interviewed in the morning followed by three in the afternoon.

The interviews ended at about five o'clock. They were all summoned at about seven to listen to the results. He said he was the last to climb up the steps of this great hall because he was so nervous.

He was delighted when they called his name as the first of the candidates appointed. There were only two successful candidates and the atmosphere was tense. He was extremely pleased and went forward to shake the hand of the Chairman and other interviewers who congratulated him.

He left the hall that evening with his colleagues who also shook hands with him. Yet, he said he could see in their eyes, the look of disgust that here was a black man being appointed to a very important job as the Chief Assistant and Senior Registrar to the Queen's Gynaecologist.

When he went to work the next day, Mr Gordon Bourne, who was the Head of Department asked him how he got on at the interview. He said it felt like he was on a rollercoaster but in any case, he had been appointed. He said Mr Bourne's face looked angry because he could not believe he would get the job.

Professor Lynch later found out that one of the candidates was the son of a friend of Mr Bourne, a consultant, based in South Africa, a Mr Neville Watham. He came to understand, an arrangement had been made between Mr Bourne and this candidate's mother for him to be seriously considered for the appointment.

So, after asking Professor Lynch a series of questions, Mr Bourne went straight to the office to confirm the veracity of what he had said. He asked his secretary which job the Professor had been appointed to and his secretary told him it was Assistant to Sir Marcus Setchell.

He said Mr Bourne came back to him to say there must have been a mistake because there was the academic job for Professor Timothy Chard and that was what Professor Lynch had been appointed to.

The Professor had already done his homework to make absolutely certain that it was Sir Marcus Setchell's job he was applying for.

Mr Bourne asked him if he would like to move on to the Professor's job instead of Sir Marcus's appointment. He said 'unfortunately no' because he thought the opportunity with Sir Marcus would open jobs and other opportunities for him in the future.

Mr Bourne, however insisted the academic job was the one he was appointed to, not Sir Marcus'. So, Professor Lynch took the piece of paper from his pocket and showed him that he had already earmarked that particular job and photocopied the right appointment regulations from the advertisement.

He said he had it in his pocket because he'd had a similar experience when he was applying for Sir Edward Tuckwell's appointment as a House Officer. So, he never forgot that he had to be vigilant and know exactly which job he was applying for so there would be no confusion.

In spite of them trying to relocate his position, he stood firmly for the job he had applied to. Mr Watham, who apparently had been promised the job was allocated to the academic job in Hackney and the Mothers.

Professor Lynch was surprised that someone who was his boss and mentor, and with whom he worked so well with and was close to could now want to take this opportunity from him. He said he could not understand it. And as he told me this story, he still seemed genuinely confused at what had happened. It appeared he was still trying to answer these questions.

At work, Mr Setchell was kind and asked him to make an appointment to go and see him and discuss his style of practice and requirements.

They worked out a programme of work which Professor Lynch said he followed. Mr Setchell asked if he would like to assist him when he operated on private patients in Harley Street. Of course, that would give him the opportunity to learn how to run a private practice when he became a consultant.

He said he could never fault Sir Marcus Setchell for the care he took of him and the advice he gave him even after he became a consultant.

Professor Lynch was fastidious in his work and he was interested in teaching and educating his junior staff. This apparently reached Sir Marcus' ears as the junior registrars and staff gave a good account of his surgical practices and how he supported their work.

Professor Lynch said this was a busy employment because Sir Marcus Setchell was a highly sought-after Gynaecological Consultant.

Sir Marcus took him to many outside functions to mingle with the rich and famous, like the Society of the Apothecaries in London where Professor Lynch became a Freeman of the City.

After He became a consultant, he was promoted from a Yeoman of the City of London to a Livery Man of the City of London when he was awarded the Freedom of the City which he still has.

In his second year, he was able to work with an eminent gynaecological cancer surgeon. He was extremely good and well known in the gynaecological field. His name was Mr John Shepherd. Mr Shepherd helped him with advice when he became a consultant and came up once to help him with a cancer patient in Milton Keynes.

He enjoyed his position as Senior Registrar at Barts until he saw an advert for a consultant appointment in the Oxford region to work for Professor, Sir Alex Turnbull's team.

Professor Lynch believes he holds the United Kingdom's record for being trained by the most Knighted Bachelors in his career:

The first was Sir Joseph Rothblatt in his first year of medical school, a

Jewish Professor from Poland;

The second Sir Edward Tuckwell, the Queens General Surgeon in his first post-graduate year;

Then Sir John Chalsery, Senior House Officer in surgery, who was also Lord Mayor of London, in his second post-graduate year;

Then Sir Alex Turnbull in Oxford where he was Junior Registrar in Obstetrics and Gynaecology;

Followed by Sir James Fraser in Southampton to whom he was Registrar;

Finally, he worked for Sir Marcus Setchell, the Queen's Gynaecologist in 1981 to 1983.

Also, at the very start of his training as a doctor, in his first year, he was trained by an eminent *Nobel Prize Winner*, Professor Sir John Wright who taught him medical physics.

He is extremely proud of this record and is always ready to share it and list the eminent men he trained under.

It therefore beggars belief that Professor Lynch did not himself end up with a Knighthood.

13

THE ROUNDABOUT TOWN

Professor Lynch described moving to Milton Keynes, known as the *'town of many roundabouts and concrete cows'* as a great dilemma because although he could have continued to stay in London, there were many others like him, and he felt like a small fish in a big pond.

Milton Keynes, however, offered him more opportunity to do more creative and exciting things. Moving to Milton Keynes would mean he did not take up the two years appointment in Hackney and The Mothers Hospital after his job with Sir Marcus.

He knew he had been well trained and had every credential to be appointed a Consultant in the United Kingdom. Nevertheless, he knew these were not the only criteria to become a consultant. One had to be in the right place at the right time.

It was on a Saturday afternoon, the summer of 1983 in the doctor's room at Barts he stumbled across the British Medical Journal job advertisement.

He picked up the article and read that Consultants/Senior Registrars were being invited to apply for jobs in the Oxford region based in Milton Keynes.

He made enquiries from his colleagues and they said Milton Keynes was a new city and the hospital had just been built. They said the population was made up of young people and the hospital was under the direction of the Oxford deanery.

He had worked for Sir Alex Turnbull as his Registrar so he felt he should give him a ring and find out what plans had been made for Milton Keynes' development. He rang Professor Turnbull who invited him to come and discuss the position.

Little did he know that in fact, Sir Alex Turnbull was in charge of all the gynaecological and obstetrics facilities in Milton Keynes, so he was the appropriate person to talk to.

When he met him, they had a nice day reminiscing about Professor Lynch's days at Oxford and what he was doing at the moment in London. Sir Alex gave him detailed information about the plans for Milton Keynes.

Sir Alex Turnbull had already received many enquiries from good candidates who had been recommended by colleagues he knew. He said it should not put him off and he should go ahead and apply.

He went back to London with a heavy heart because he knew deep down, he had all the best qualifications but being black was always a factor with these appointments.

He did not let it put him off though and he discussed it with his consultants, Mr Gordon Bourne who was the Head of Department and Sir Marcus Setchell who was his direct consultant.

He also wrote to Professor Sir James Fraser who was his supervisor in general surgery when he was in Southampton. He said he would support his application and wrote him a nice letter of support.

He felt a little bit reassured because he had good people supporting him, as well as his outstanding qualifications.

The day of the interview came, it was December 13th. There were seven candidates shortlisted and he was one of them. He was the first candidate called in because of his name which came early in the alphabet.

He said he was properly grilled at the interview but fortunately he had worked at Oxford and knew about the developments going on in Milton Keynes.

He had done some research on the statistics of the population structure of Milton Keynes and he had found out 67% of women were under the age of thirty-five. He knew the statistics of women in the younger age group would be appropriate to consider in relation to obstetrics and gynaecology.

He said he thought he performed well in the interview though he was by no means certain. He was delighted when the interview finished.

The secretary came out and called out his name as the first candidate who had been successful. He said the joy he felt was the same sensation as passing his Fellowship exam in Edinburgh.

Two other consultants were appointed out of the seven Interviewees. One was Scottish from Glasgow and the other was an English doctor from Leeds. They hugged each other warmly and arranged to meet in London for dinner to celebrate their appointments.

The Scottish doctor was Mr Graham McQune who had worked for the President of the College of Gynaecologists in the past. The English doctor was Mr Rupert Fawdry, well experienced and had worked in many interesting places both within the UK and abroad.

As he was the one living in London, he found a convenient place for them to meet. They had a good dinner in celebration of their appointments.

They compared notes as to what training they had each received so they knew how much they would each contribute to the new appointment and the new department.

They agreed to meet in Milton Keynes later to discuss the plans for their service to this new community and this new city.

Mr Fawdry confirmed from independent research, it was a city with a young population who had mainly come from London, Glasgow, and Birmingham and who were mostly working-class families.

This presented a challenge to the practice at that time as clinics were held in hospitals. They decided to change the pattern of practice of clinics held in the district. They would take their services to the population rather than have the population come to the hospital in order to reduce the issues of transport difficulties and 'DNAs' (did not appear) and so on.

They divided up the clinics and the catchment area into three parts. Professor Lynch was allocated the North, McQune was the East, and Fawdry was the West.

The next thing they decided was what kind of practice they would individually offer. They all did everything but for specialist cases they shared responsibility according to expertise and training.

They decided Professor Lynch would oversee the surgical aspect because of his training and expertise- so he did all the gynaecological surgeries and complications.

Mr McQune saw all the high-risk pregnancies and also ran the fertility clinic. Mr Fawdry did mainly Uro Gynaecology and oversaw IT and patient communications.

He developed a new patients' record system which the patient would carry with them. The advantage of which would be that wherever she went, she could present the document to the hospital in her locality and they would understand her management.

This was quite unique because patient's records at the time were kept in hospitals. That system became successful and is still practised today.

He said he was unsure about how he would be received as the first black Consultant at Milton Keynes hospital, however, he integrated well into the hospital.

The Chairman of Milton Keynes hospital was also the Chairman of the appointments committee when he was appointed, so he remembered him and tried to make him feel welcome as did his wife.

Personally, I heard about how some of his colleagues sabotaged his work and tried to make him fail. They were not all as rosy to him as he makes out. He was successful and good at what he did and so they could not mess him up easily, but it was not for want of some people trying.

Recently I tried to get a reference from one of the Senior Consultant Gynaecologists at the hospital, whom Professor had trained and of whom he spoke highly and believed the Doctor would support his nomination for a Queen's Award. The doctor was rude, unhelpful and dismissive, almost acted like he did not even know Professor Lynch.

From conversations I have heard with some of his past mentees and colleagues, backbiting and sabotage went on a lot without Professor's knowledge and even if he did realise it, his default was to ignore it and *'Walk softly among the Tulips'*.

He said he and his colleagues worked to move the hospital forward in this new environment. The demand was high and the responsibility was outstanding. They had a lot to do and had to work out of hours.

Funding was limited because it had to be shared amongst other specialties who were also conducting staff appointments for their departments.

In response to this situation, Professor Lynch set up the Myrtle Peach Trust, a charity trust to allow women to attend to have treatment if referred by their GPs as outpatients. Through this trust, they were able to raise funds to purchase a microscope and laser.

He recruited the help of a local, famous celebrity and Jazz singer, Dame Cleo Laine and her late husband John Dankworth who ran a local entertainment centre called The Stables.

He invited Dame Cleo Lane to be one of his patrons. She and her husband did a tremendous job fundraising for this worthy cause. They organised performances for the charity and raised a significant amount of money with which they could purchase this vital equipment. He said he remains indebted to them for this purpose.

Students from Barts in London came to do their outreach training with Professor Lynch in Milton Keynes. He had a good reputation at Barts for his teaching skills and training so his colleagues there used Milton Keynes as one of the training centres for the medical students and junior doctors.

They organised a cricket match between St Barts and the Great Linford Cricket Club where he was now a member to raise funds for the Myrtle Peach Trust.

They ran the match on a Saturday. The Barts team won and they had a wonderful day and raised over a thousand pounds which was good money in those days. They bought a microscope for cervical cancer screening, but they did not have enough money for the laser, so fundraising continued through the newspaper and other avenues.

He had his students from Barts help him by sharing leaflets and going on matches to raise the funds. They finally raised enough funds to buy the laser.

The minister of health, Mr Newton, at the time, was invited to come and present the laser equipment that he had raised funds for to Milton Keynes. They had a small function with him doing the presentation.

It was also attended by Mr Luing Cowly the Chairman of the Health Authority who also became a patron of the Myrtle Peach Trust, and Dame Rosemary Rue from Oxford.

According to Professor Lynch, the Myrtle Peach Trust was named so after Mrs Myrtle Peach, a fifty-six-year-old woman who ran a florist shop.

She was well known in Newport Pagnell for making flowers for special functions. In fact, when he bought his show house, she did the decorations for his housewarming party.

Her memory was preserved in the hospital as the Myrtle Peach Trust Foundation to help prevent other women from contracting cervical cancer due to lack of screening. Every year, they would have a dinner and dance in memory of Myrtle Peach to raise funds for the laser and colposcopy equipment.

For me, I must query the point of positive contribution when at the end of the day it cannot be recognised and rewarded.

Anyone I have spoken to about Professor Lynch and the Myrtle Peach Trust told me he was a dynamic man who raised a lot of money for the Trust and of course, by so doing saved the lives of thousands of women.

In Milton Keynes Hospital, however, I see no trace of him having been there, no recognition of his contribution to cervical cancer prevention and treatment. He might as well never have been there.

I have written to the Hospital CEO to back his nomination for a Queen's Award. I was expecting that with everything he had done, it would be an easy thing to do, but it wasn't. He said he had never worked with Professor Lynch and so could not provide a reference. But in my opinion *'he has a legacy there. Your cervical cancer trust is standing because he set it up. Does that alone not deserve your support'*?

Professor Lynch said he is pleased to say the programme continues even into his retirement because of the foundation which he had set at the outset of his appointment. He visited the hospital recently and cervical cancer treatment is still an important part of the hospital's provisions.

During his work with the Myrtle Peach Trust, he was invited to give lectures on health at the Open University. The Professors there were monitoring his work at Milton Keynes Hospital.

They paid particular attention to his fundraising activities in the community and had created a profile of him which led to a formal invitation to him to receive an Honorary Doctorate.

He said when he received the letter, he was happy and also felt particularly worthy of the award.

The work he did quickly travelled around the UK. He was invited to give many lectures to talk about how he was able to start the programme to screen women with abnormal smears. He said it was with the help of his nurses and community leaders that he became successful in this enterprise.

He said his aim was to improve the quality of service to make Milton Keynes one of the best in the UK and his two colleagues were also committed to that aim because they worked night and day and they toiled to bring up the quality of service in Milton Keynes.

The hospital boomed from scratch to becoming a well-known hospital in the UK both for its cancer work and its high-risk pregnancy care and patient note carrying work which his colleague Mr Fawdry had pioneered. They were young Consultants but often described as having outstanding intellect and ambition.

When the hospital opened, they had an influx of patients who had been going to Bedford, Northampton, Luton and Dunstable for their care. They also maintained a link with these hospitals for aspects of care that were already established with them.

At work, they established their departments with the three of them as founding Consultants: Mr Fawdry, Mr McQune and himself. They had meetings every week to discuss management plans, hear complaints and support the nurses with any difficulties and their service provision.

His speciality interest was surgery so he developed this sub-specialist interest in cancer work where his interest in cancer of the cervix was the prime subject.

In 1988, he decided to cut down on his London commitments and concentrate on moving Milton Keynes forward with education, science and development. The service they gave to their patients was exemplary and he said they raised the standards of practice without any difficulty.

The district was assigned for financing and development to the Oxford University Deanery - from education and training to service provision - all was in league and participation with the Oxford Deanery.

This link had its advantages and disadvantages. One of the advantages was that they were associated with an outstanding university. The educational ties were useful.

The disadvantage was that they did not control their own budgets. It was, however, necessary for them to have their own budgetary independence and not have a begging bowl each time they needed to improve structures and quality at Milton Keynes.

He said not many of his patients remember his name but they remember the way he presented himself, always with a flower in his button-hole and a three-piece suit with a gold chain. That was how they described him when they were in outpatients and asked in whose care they were.

Professor Lynch always liked to look smart and well turned out. Some of his colleagues would say to me *'Oh if you had seen this man in his glory days -he was a sight to behold'*. He would always say to me *'I used to look good'* and proceed to show me photographs of himself in his younger days.

That was one of the reasons he was uncomfortable when he had to stay in hospital. He was no longer in charge of when or how he dressed and he did not like that at all. He hated the hospital gown and rumpled shirts and jumpers he had to wear, because to him how one is presented and seen mattered. He liked to look dignified wherever he went.

14

OGUN COTTAGE

The hospital did not provide accommodation for the newly arrived consultants, so Professor Lynch had to visit the Council to look at areas suitable and proximal to the hospital.

He was guided by a lady in the council who directed him to the north where his practice would be with the GP surgery. The place was called Great Linford - it was near Newport Pagnell so transportation would not be a problem.

They visited the Great Linford area and saw lots of nice, newly built houses. He liked it and he said he was lucky to find himself a new show house built beside the local cricket green. He was a keen cricketer so he knew he might affiliate with the cricketers in the area.

He went into the offices of the estate agents, Brown and Merry, to enquire and he was told the show house would be sold closer to completion, but they were accepting bids for it.

He said the show house was wonderful. It had everything including electric blinds and a pond in the garden around the boundaries of the cricket pitch itself. He imagined watching cricket matches from the lounge.

On enquiring about the price, he was told it was expensive - a hundred and ten thousand pounds for the four-bedroom detached house.

The local pub was on the other side of the cricket green. There were other similar houses quite adjacent on the same street, Marsh Drive.

He discovered those houses belonged to some of the other consultants at Milton Keynes Hospital - there was a radiologist Dr Al-Haque from Pakistan, Mr Robin Suter from Glasgow, and others whose names he could no longer remember. It was clear he'd have good company as well as a pleasant environment.

On the other side of the estate was a recording studio where Mick Jagger recorded some of his music. In between, they had the local community centre which was quite noisy at times but not unbearable.

The Professor loved his residence which he called the 'Ogun Cottage' at Great Linford. Ogun is part of his name, 'Balogun'. He explained that historically, 'Ogun' means the leader or chief. Its origin is Yoruba from Nigeria. The Balogun is the leader of the group, the one around whom the villagers would congregate for advice and direction.

He said when he bought his house in Great Linford, he had sold his flat at the Barbican where he lived while working at Barts as a Senior Registrar and Clinical Assistant to the Queen's gynaecologist.

The Barbican was close to the hospital and he had sold it for forty-six thousand pounds and it was then easy to raise the rest of the money to secure the show house.

Having bought the show house in Great Linford, he had to decide about travelling to Harley Street in London as opposed to home consulting in Great Linford.

At Harley Street, he had a good reputation and he had a lot of private patients. Having worked as Assistant to the Queen's Gynaecologist, he had a lot of patients associated with that contact and they wanted to keep seeing him so he had to keep the practice going.

Three months after he moved into Ogun Cottage, he decided to have a housewarming party and celebrate the opening of the Department.

As his house was close to the cricket ground, there was ample space to hold the party without annoying the neighbours. In fact, some of his neighbours attended the party.

First, he said he contacted his now-deceased colleague, Mr Quashie Foster-Jones who had the famous restaurant previously mentioned called 'Toddies'.

He also recruited the help of publicans for the party who had a pub near his medical school in Clerkenwell Road where Barts Medical College was located. Their names were Mr and Mrs Newton. They were an influential Orthodox Jewish couple.

He said one could get anything they wanted on earth from the pub. It was frequented by everyone from bank managers, city dignitaries, influential people, to people who worked at the Smithfield market, like the butchers, fruit sellers, and so on.

Above the pub was the Clerkenwell Masonic Centre and the Masons would also visit the pub following their meetings. It was a well located, influential and diverse pub. Professor went there regularly when he was working at Barts doing his training and he and the Newtons became friendly.

When one of their employees had a knife accident, he dealt with it at the casualty unit at Barts. He said there was nothing he wanted they would not help him with if he asked.

When he was leaving Barts to move to Milton Keynes as a consultant they were pleased for him and gave him a party in the bar which was well received and attended.

They were the couple whom he said commissioned and presented him with the engagement ring he gave to his wife.

When he had his housewarming party in Milton Keynes, the Newtons brought him wine and all the beverages he needed for the party in a big van. The party was well supplied, with magnificent food of all types from Mr Quashie Jones' Toddies and wines from Mr and Mrs Newton.

He described the party as 'magnificent'. It started on Friday about 10pm and finished on Sunday morning when most people departed.

They had a friendly cricket match on the Saturday to raise some money for The Myrtle Peach Trust.

It was described by some of the GPs as the best party they had ever attended and maybe the best party in memory. He said he cannot recall any other occasion where all members of staff of the hospital were so connected.

The Chairman of the hospital authority was one of their special guests, the late Mr Luing Cowley. He was also the Mayor of Milton Keynes at the time.

His students from Barts came up to give him a hand and help with the organisation of the party and stayed the weekend in the cricket grounds with makeshift camps and tents.

He said the party set him up nicely as not only an obstetrician/gynaecologist but also one who had the ability to bring people together since people from the various departments were in attendance.

15

LOVING JULIE

Once appointed, they now had the duty of staffing their departments with secretaries to help the departments progress with proper record keeping and communications. They put out advertisements for secretaries.

The first group to attend was for Mr McQune, the high-risk pregnancy doctor. The appointed secretary was around forty-five years old, with a lot of experience.

They also appointed Mr McQune as the clinical director of the department. He was keen to liaise with management to ensure they had the required support to run the departments.

The next appointment was for Professor Lynch's secretary. She was very experienced but unfortunately had glandular fever and could not attend.

She had Harley Street experience working for an eye specialist in London and wanted to work for the new hospital in Milton Keynes. Instead, they had to appoint somebody else in that group whom he said was adequate but not outstanding.

His other colleague, Mr Fawdry, advertised for an IT person to progress with his caseloads. A very nice, chirpy lady from London called Ms Julie Klinner was appointed. She had previously worked for an eye specialist and was acquainted with private practice.

This was the same nurse who was supposed to come for Professor Lynch's interview but could not attend on that day. He spotted that she was intelligent, knowledgeable, and was used to private practice in London. This appealed to him even though she was not his secretary.

He said he wondered perhaps, if there had been another reason for her not attending his original interview. So, he stopped her in the corridor one day and told her he felt she had not come to his interview as she did not like him and because he was black. She said this was not the case and it was because she was ill. She told him she was used to working with people from diverse ethnic backgrounds whilst she was in London. So, he was convinced she was genuinely ill and unable to come.

I am not convinced though. Do people not reschedule interviews for jobs they want? Could she not do the same? This is our first encounter with Julie and it seems he has already fallen for her.

She continued to work for Mr Fawdry but he goes out of his way to hire her to do his private practice work for his London practice because he was still consulting for 152 Harley Street.

He said she was efficient and did all his bookings, appointments, and surgical lists. This, I guess was at the beginning of her appointment because I learnt that later on she barely helped him at all.

He said he and Julie would plan private patient appointments and lists in his house in Great Linford. He said his department had become well known for its cancer work and maternity care, and his private practice boomed in London with the help of his secretary, Julie. She worked with him at the weekends and would remind him of what he had to do for the week.

He thought she was good and their relationship blossomed from there. At the time, he was a single man and she was at that point engaged to an Englishman. He said he was able to win her over and subsequently she became his girlfriend, which progressed to them getting married and having a family together.

Professor Lynch told me Julie's mother was an English country lady who came from a farming family. Her father was German but had established himself in the UK in agriculture.

He said he and Julie had been going strong from 1984 when he came to Milton Keynes to 1986 when they got married.

They got engaged at St Paul's Cathedral in London. They had gone there for some reason, though he cannot remember what it was.

Whilst kneeling for prayers, he took her hand and put this beautiful hand-crafted ring on her finger. At first, she thought he had picked it up from the floor or from someone sitting in the front chair.

When he told me this story, I couldn't help but wonder why a potential fiancée of an eminent consultant gynaecologist/obstetrician would think that he would steal a ring from someone else. What was her understanding of this man? How did she see him?

If I was the Professor, this is where all the alarm bells would start ringing, but in love the heart rarely listens to the head and the Professor's desire to prove himself worthy of the women he loved like he did with Maria, the French nurse, seemed to be at play again.

He said when she saw the box that the ring was in, however, she realised it was specially made for her. His idea was to get the blessing for the ring before he passed it on to her.

He described the ring as a *'magnificent ring of sapphire and two diamonds'* made by the famous jewellers Mappin and Webb. The ring had been specially commissioned for him by his friends, the Newtons who owned a pub close to the hospital and with whom he had gotten close.

Since he had been made a Freeman of the City of London, this gave him some privileges he could utilise when his wedding day came. He applied for his ceremony to take place at St Bartholomew's the Great which was next to the hospital. He could have the reception at the Honourable Artillery Company on Finsbury Pavement in the City.

He said they had a brilliant wedding and though both of his parents were absent he knew their spirits were with them.

His mother was still alive but could not attend and so her sister came instead. He had lost his father in his childhood, so his uncle came in his stead.

His uncle was the Honourable John Anthony Roberts, QC in the United Kingdom. He was the first black QC in London and he was made a Commander of the British Empire.

He had practiced in the UK and had sometimes represented the UK as Governor General in certain parts of Africa. He had also served as a High Commissioner for the UK. He had been decorated as a CBE for services to the United Kingdom. Professor Lynch described him as a *'sound and bright individual'*.

He invited his English teacher who had taught him in Sierra Leone but now lived in the village of Dean in England. She was an English lady called Mrs Elizabeth Hirst. She had taught him his favourite subject and so Mrs Hirst was personal to him and he said it was good to see her again after so many years.

He said the vicar predicted that their wedding would last. They had a lovely service which was well attended and the reception was good. The gallery was occupied by the minstrels of the Honourable Artillery Company who played the music for the reception. He said everything went like clockwork and it was exciting.

They planned to go on honeymoon to Marbella in Spain. At that time, he had a Porsche 928 S2 and drove from the UK to Santander and eventually to their destination in Marbella, a lovely golfing retreat.

He said Julia promised to help him with driving from the UK to Spain, but each time her turn came to take over the driving she said she wasn't feeling up to it.

They stopped in Madrid and other places along the way to refresh themselves. They enjoyed the hotels on the way and had a good time. Coming back, they stopped as many times as possible till they got back to Milton Keynes. It was a pleasant honeymoon and he said he would always remember it.

When they discovered his wife was pregnant for the first time, he said he felt anxiety and panic: anxiety because it was his first child; panic, because as an obstetrician, he was aware of all the things that could go wrong. Fortunately, she had a normal and uncomplicated pregnancy and delivery.

He had to choose the best obstetrician apart from himself for her care. He chose Mr Anthony Silverstone of University College, London. All his children were born at the Portland Hospital for Women and Children.

Both Fergie and Princess Anne had their children there. He was also doing some private consultancy work at this hospital at the time when his children were born. His wife was always well-treated, and he said he was grateful to the staff for that.

He told me their first child was born in 1988, Joshua a male child who went to private school in Bedford and eventually to Imperial College, London where he did medicine and is now training as a GP.

Sarah, their next child was born two years later and went to school in Bedford and works in Insurance.

Emily was born two years after Sarah. She studied English at King's College London and is now a qualified teacher in Milton Keynes after completing her diploma in education. He said his last child Isabelle is training as a tax inspector with the Inland Revenue.

As a family, they would go to Wales to a timeshare bungalow they had in Talgarth. Now he is divorced, his wife has taken that part of his properties whilst he had the flat in Bedford to enable the children to live there whilst they were still at school in the area. It reduced the inconvenience of travelling to school from Milton Keynes.

He has now sold the flat in Bedford to fund the purchase of his current premises. They also had a place in Portugal, in Place De Algarve which was a famous golfing area.

He said they were happy living in their seven-bedroom house in Little Linford. He used to invite his colleagues from America to come and work with him on research projects and they would stay in his house. He also ran his private surgery in Milton Keynes from the outbuilding on his property which was appreciated by the patients since it provided privacy.

Professor always says he regrets the breakup of his family and though he puts on a brave face, deep down in himself he feels sad. He said *'I did nothing bad, it was a simple misunderstanding'*.

I remember seeing a video interview of him where he told the interviewer he had asked his wife's permission before attending the interview. I remember wondering why he needed his wife's permission to do an interview. But in another interview, he said the most important thing to him was his family and all his achievements faded in comparison. He said he felt all his achievements would be meaningless if he did not have his family, so I know he really did love his wife and children.

He calls his divorce the second tragedy of his life. He said his divorce was based on a misunderstanding with his wife whom he loved very much.

He says when he teaches, he always impresses upon recipients that there is nothing one can get in life as an acquisition that would be of more value, than a good and happy family.

'I was one of the most respected people in my profession, I had invented the B- Lynch, I had done everything one could think of to improve oneself in the profession. In the end, it was my profession that brought me down. As I pursued another discovery and success, I lost my family'.

They had to sell Linford Court, their seven-bedroom house, which the children loved and where he had hosted fellows who came to do their research and move to a flat where he now lives with nothing to show, but photographs, for all the wonderful work he had done and the family he had had.

He said he believed in the Latin quotation which says, *'dum spiro spero'* — *'whilst I live, I hope'*. I wonder if he's still hoping for a reconciliation with his wife but as he'd already told me he no longer had the money or the capacity to make more at the moment, so he had nothing to offer her which made a reconciliation unlikely.

Like me, he hoped the autobiography would make money, so maybe that was the hope that would change his life and make him rich and relevant and desirable again.

When we were sending out the invitations to the book launch, he said I should send one to his ex-wife. I asked him why, but he said she might want to attend. Yes, the hope that she would see him successful and relevant again.

16

THE ACADEMIC

Professor Lynch was a true academic. He committed his life to these pursuits. Even in his old age as I was working with him on his autobiography, he was still travelling around the world teaching.

In the year we worked together, he visited Mexico which he loved as he said they treated him like Royalty and Saudi Arabia. Put Professor Lynch in front of an audience and give him a microphone and he would be in his element.

His unit was popular in the college for training excellence. He began to have students who were not at Barts apply to come to him. For example, students from St Mary's Hospital who were encouraged to contact him by their colleagues at Barts. If he was able to accommodate them, he would accept them for training.

He was appointed by the College of Gynaecologists to be the district tutor for postgraduate studies.

His devotion to education and training was so outstanding, the National Health Service gave him the Merit Award which brought some financial rewards for him as well.

He said it brought a lot of responsibility for not just service provision but for the training and education of doctors who came his way.

As the clinical tutor for the district appointed by the Royal College of Obstetricians and Gynaecology, he organised the post-graduate training programme as well as the under graduates from St Bartholomew's Hospital in London.

As a keen teacher, he introduced and monitored his students in research skills. He was nominated for the Surgical Trainer of the Year by the Smith & Nephew foundation. He was one of the shortlisted candidates after many interviews, visits, and scrutiny. His students and junior staff supported him and he was a runner-up in the final award.

He said the surgical training experience he provided was first-class because he was trained as a general surgeon by six Knights Bachelors of the medical profession.

These eminent men of talent taught him a great deal which he passed on through his own teaching to make his trainees better doctors, not only in skill but in their attitude to patients, their conduct in research and above all, to be good members of the community.

He received a letter of invitation to attend an assessment interview at Cranfield. Before accepting the appointment, he said he had a discussion with his wife, who was then looking after four children, to see if he might have time to devote to it in addition to what he was doing at Milton Keynes Hospital. She agreed with him that he should do it and if it got too much he could always resign.

His first research project at the university was to describe the pathways in immune ageing and regeneration. Since he was a gynaecologist, the menopause was important to him and this aspect of immunology in aging and regeneration was useful.

Secondly, he collaborated and worked on a simple model system enabling human CD34- the differentiation towards human T cells in cancer management. This was up his street because it dealt with cancer work and the main system of cancer proliferation. This article was well received by the cancer institute.

On the academic side, they explored comprehensive teaching methods in postpartum haemorrhage (PPH) for foundation and internship doctors. He was strong in this area so the design for the protocol of this subject was simple. This also became a publication of interest towards the training of young doctors.

Finally, he encouraged the university to explore his recent invention of the B-Lynch transverse compression suture for the control of postpartum haemorrhage from placenta premia bleeding. This became a major subject of interest.

These four research projects gave value to his role as visiting Professor of Cranfield University, Department of Health Science. He named his collaborating colleague as Professor Dr Richard Aspinal with whom he worked well.

During this appointment at Cranfield, he came home one evening after a tiring day from a long operating list at the Milton Keynes Hospital. A phone call came through from a colleague, with whom he had trained at St Barts Hospital. He was called Professor Terrence Kealy.

He said he was surprised to get his call as he had not seen or heard from him for a long time, since the mid-90s. They were both Senior Registrars at St Barts Hospital.

Kealy was in general medicine, and he was a bright individual working for the Professor of medicine at Barts, whilst he was at the obstetrics and gynaecology department as senior registrar to the Queen's gynaecologist.

They were friends and had done collaborative research together on hypertension in pregnancy and various other subjects of interest.

Unbeknown to Professor Lynch, Kealy had secured an appointment in academia at Buckingham University and rose to the position of Vice Chancellor.

He said he remembered him as being politically active whist studying and practicing medicine and was closely involved with the late Margaret Thatcher who became the Chancellor of Buckingham University.

The phone call was for them to have dinner and talk about academic programmes and prospects for Milton Keynes Hospital. Little did Professor know he had the same interest as him that Milton Keynes Hospital would achieve university status.

They met in a restaurant, called Robinson's in Newport Pagnell and reflected and reminisced on old times. Among the discussions they had was to see how they could escalate Milton Keynes Hospital to academic status.

The bottom line as he said he understood it, was that this was going to be a private university exercise. It would reduce the duration of training from five years to four years and create a curriculum which would cover all the subjects and training in that time. Terrence was able to sell the idea to the Department of Education.

Professor had a meeting with the Chief Executive of the hospital who was agreeable and could see the benefit this association with the university would bring and the encouragement of staff to come and work and be educated at the hospital.

Fortunately, the Professor's colleagues in all the major specialties at Milton Keynes hospital agreed to participate in the training of junior doctors over four years instead of five.

So once plans were underway, he and Terrence were happy to carry on the collaboration between Milton Keynes Hospital and Buckingham University. At this point they were able to secure funds to create a good post graduate academic centre well designed for this purpose.

It brought some degree of status and educational improvement to the hospital.

When he retired from the hospital, Mr Douglas Mcqueny took his place in leadership in the university work with the hospital.

The Professor said he remembered well before this time, at the peak of his career, he was interviewed by an Open University representative on how he came to be in Milton Keynes and what he saw as the future of Milton Keynes Hospital. He remembered saying to the interviewer *'I would do my best to see that the hospital received university status. I was pleased to see my dream come through'.*

He told me he hoped it prospers and becomes an example of how medical training can be conducted over a slightly shorter time with the proper organisation and goodwill.

Professor was invited by the European Endoscopic Surgery Unit based in Paris in the 90s to become a member of faculty to teach gynaecological endoscopy.

He had had the opportunity to train in laparoscopic surgery which did not exist in Milton Keynes at the time.

He learnt the technique as one of the four consultants from the United Kingdom to introduce the practice in the UK. There was one from London, Liverpool, Oxford and Milton Keynes respectively.

The purpose of keyhole surgery was to reduce hospital stay and have a more precise observation of surgical technique. The cut was very small and so recovery was much quicker.

Professor introduced the technique in Milton Keynes, but of course, he was in competition for resources with other departments. He persevered to show that this brought good quality care to their patients and to gynaecological practice. From then on, he carried out most of the gynaecological procedures by keyhole surgery.

He was invited to become a member of the Faculty of the European Union Society of Keyhole Surgeons which included Germans, French, English, Scottish, and other European professors- all the leading lights were there.

He described this as *'An immense experience not only in meeting colleagues from Europe with similar interests but also in training young doctors, communicating with colleagues and updating experiences.'*

17
MY NAME IS ON IT

Professor Lynch is famous for inventing the B-Lynch Suture, a gynaecological procedure used to stop haemorrhaging at childbirth.

This Procedure is used in hospitals and taught in universities around the globe.

On social media, a young man contacted me once to say he was being taught the procedure in University. At the hospital when he was admitted recently one of the doctors came up to see him and said to me 'I have just used the *'B-Lynch Suture'* on a patient downstairs'. A friend of mine in a hospital in Canada said to me recently he could see they had written B-Lynch Suture on the board which meant an operation was being carried out using the method.

When I said it was the only invention in gynaecology and obstetrics in one hundred years, his former boss, Sir Marcus Setchell said that was debateable. I believe it is the only invention in at least fifty years if not a hundred.

It is an invention which has saved the lives of millions of women worldwide.

So, of course, it had to be something we discussed, and I asked him to tell me the events which led to the invention.

He told me that on 29th November 1989, he was a consultant obstetric and gynaecological surgeon at Milton Keynes Hospital. He had returned home from a busy day, quite exhausted. He went to sleep quite early and in the middle of the night, he had a dream.

In this dream, he received a call from the Milton Keynes Hospital emergency department who told him a patient of his from the district of Stony Stratford had been involved in a road traffic accident. Without any delay, he got dressed and went to the hospital arriving almost at the same time as the ambulance.

When he got to the casualty, he saw an unconscious woman who was thirty-eight weeks pregnant. She was unconscious but the anaesthetist had been able to maintain her breathing.

He listened to her belly, the baby's heartbeat was barely heard, so even though he was in his suit he asked for a pair of gloves and a knife and painted her abdomen with iodine antiseptic. He made three incisions on her tummy - one up and down and two across and delivered the baby.

They then had difficulties stopping the bleeding. He did all the standard manoeuvres to accomplish haemostasis and stop the bleeding but it failed.

He said something came to his mind that he should use his braces to compress the womb down which he did and it stopped the bleeding. The mother recovered and so did the baby.

He was delighted and woke up from his sleep with this miracle dream. He hurried to the bathroom and grabbed a piece of paper to write it down.

He said he usually kept paper in the toilets in case there was a phone call and he needed to write something down urgently. He wrote down the summary of this observation.

He said his wife was annoyed because he woke her up and was scribbling away in the toilet in the middle of the night.

When he went to the hospital the next day, he transcribed his observation of the entire incident in his computer with a drawing. He told his colleagues and they all laughed at him and one said he should not be taking work home and disturbing his wife's sleep.

Six months later, one of his colleagues Rupert was performing a Caesarean section. The patient was bleeding and he had difficulty stopping it. He rang Professor Lynch at home to come and help him which he did.

Professor said to him, "*You know what, six months ago, I dreamt of a technique of compressing the uterus with suture, in that case it was my braces and it stopped. Why don't we try using a suture called Catgut.'*

Prior to this, he had not mentioned his idea again as he had been laughed at and he had felt annoyed because he was not taken seriously. At this moment, with Rupert, however, it made sense to use it.

This Catgut suture is now banned from practice because they say it is made from animal gut and may cause mad cow disease. However, progress must begin somewhere and in this case all those years ago, it worked.

They carried out the procedure in exactly the same way he had dreamt using his braces and the bleeding stopped. The patient lived after losing fifteen or twenty pints of blood.

Her husband was worried he would lose his wife and gave Professor a hug when he came out of the theatre. He also gave the department Two Thousand Pounds as a gift to buy any equipment they wanted. The ultrasound machine was useful in obstetrics, so the money went towards purchasing it.

Professor said he collected cases of similar incidents around postpartum haemorrhage and wrote a paper after collecting about seven cases. He called the paper the *'B-Lynch Operation for Postpartum Haemorrhage'* and sent it to the British Journal.

The editors were not happy for him to have his name on it. They were keen to just call it the *'treatment of postpartum haemorrhage'* but they did not know he had consulted a lawyer about stopping anyone else calling the procedure by their own name following his publication.

After being rejected by the British Journal, the American Journal were very pleased and wanted to publish it, so he told the British Journal authorities the Americans were happy to publish this miracle technique. The British Journal then relented and agreed to publish it which it did, seven years after he first invented it. He added *'The procedure which came as a miracle to me in 1989 became an established procedure in 1997'*.

Professor said that twenty years after this procedure had been in use worldwide, the World Health Organisation published a survey from various parts of the world on maternity care. It stated that the lives of over two million women around the world had been saved through the effective application of and successful treatment of postpartum haemorrhage using the B Lynch procedure.

Further literature has been published on this technique and Professor has been invited to many countries to run workshops and teach doctors. Every hospital in the world has his technique on display for teaching and education. He has been to over fifty countries in the world teaching this technique - United States, many countries in Europe, India, Pakistan, Japan, South America, and many others.

This technique was so popular and effective, he was invited by three of his senior colleagues to write a text book on postpartum haemorrhage, a 460-page textbook for which he recruited several authors to contribute to all aspects of what they know about managing postpartum haemorrhage.

The book was launched in October 1996 by her Royal Highness the Princess Royal, Princess Anne, at the Royal Society of Medicine

London. Professor was the principal speaker and the senior editor of this textbook called the *'Management of Postpartum Haemorrhage - Comprehensive Account'*.

The book launch was well attended - the President of the Royal College of Gynaecologists was in attendance and the introductory speech was given by Sir Marcus Setchell, the former gynaecologist to the Queen. They also had the Senior Professor from Harvard University, the late Professor Louis Keith from America. Also in attendance was the regional director of the World Health Organisation Professor Louise Sambo.

The book launch dinner was held at the Athenaeum Club in London in Pall Mall, a highly reputable society for education and invention. Professor added that the textbook has benefited so many institutions in the world and saved the lives of many women.

From the moment we started writing the autobiography Professor told me he wanted to launch the book at the Athenaeum Club. When we completed the book, I made sure I called the Club and booked the launch event there to ensure his wish was fulfilled.

In 2016, he was nominated for the Nobel Peace Prize for his invention by colleagues from Poland, Ukraine and the United States of America. Although he did not win, he appreciated the effort made by his colleagues who put him forward.

He said he is pleased that before he dies, he knows he has made a contribution to science which will benefit people for years to come.

The late Dr Louis G. Keith Professor Emeritus in Obstetrics and Gynaecology, from the USA who was a close colleague of Professor Lynch and with whom he co-authored a textbook on past-partum haemorrhage made this comment in a video interview, *'Well he has his name on it, what more is there to say?'*

THE END

EPILOGUE

THE PROFESSOR AND I

When we started writing his autobiography, I was at Professor Lynch's house about five days a week for eight straight months.

I watched him go through his battle with cancer. I came to know him, or at least as much as one is available to be known. But I came to love him and cared deeply for him as though he was my father.

We settled into a routine and he looked forward to me turning up at his house at 10am every weekday for two, three or four hours and some evenings. It gave him a reason to get up and get changed in the morning.

He rarely had visitors. One of his friends, Javid who went to the same Lodge as him and I were his most frequent guests. He had a problem with his back which he could not operate on because of the chance of paralysis so his mobility was limited. He was in the house most of the time by himself watching TV. His third daughter, Emily lived with him but, she worked, had evening activities or was in her room when she was home.

He, however, loved to go out so we went on several lunches and dinner dates with his friends, colleagues or people he had helped who visited him from all over the country or the world.

I also accompanied him to a charity book launch by Sir Marcus and the lunch reunion at the Great Hall I mentioned earlier.

I invited him to a ball in Milton Keynes called the *'Wakanda Ball'* which he attended with his childhood sweetheart, Monica. Monica had come back into his life after more than thirty years and they were now good friends. When he was sick in hospital, she not only visited him but called almost every day to check on him. She still cooks and sends him food.

We started writing in November 2018. By August 2019 we had a first draft which I hired an editor to look at. That meant the visits to Professor Lynch started to reduce.

When the first edit came back from the editor, I returned to Professor Lynch to go through the suggested changes and make the required amendments. Then the book went back to the editor. During this time, I was seeing him less.

Following the second edit from the editor we went over the entire book again page by page, checking spellings of names of people, confirming dates, clarifying statements. When he was happy, I sent it back to the editor.

By now he was getting tired and fed up, I think. When the third edit returned from the editor, I took him the printed copy. He was surprised to see the finished product but he said he did not want to read it. He said he was tired of reading the book.

At this point I no longer needed to see him. I had the photographs he had given me to scan for the book and other work to do such as organising the Forward, cover design, book publishing and launch.

One Monday morning after a meeting in the city, I was on my way to my studio but I decided I would give him a call. His speech sounded drawn and not quite himself so instead of going to work I decided I would go and see him.

When I got there, he seemed depressed and withdrawn and his speech was slurred and slow. I realised he was not himself so I settled down to stay with him for a while.

He said he wanted some money from the bank. I usually got money out for him but as I had not done so in a while, I had forgotten his PIN number. He told me what he thought it was and I went to the cash point to get him some money.

At the cash point, the PIN number was wrong. This was the first time I had seen Professor Lynch forget a number in twelve months. We had just gone through his entire autobiography and he had remembered all the dates in it. I was stunned.

I went back home to collect him so we could go to the bank and change his PIN number. The bank was just five minutes from his house.

He had his walking frame and he stood up. In slow motion, it seemed to me, he started falling sideways towards me with the table behind him. I tried to hold on to him but he is such a big man physically, I could not hold him and he fell to the floor. I tried to pick him up off the floor but did not have the strength to do so.

I had to call my husband who left work and came to help me pick him up. We helped him onto his scooter and we went to the bank. We changed his PIN number to a number easy for me to remember and which he promised would be easy for him to remember. Then we went back home.

Once he was seated back in his chair, I went out and bought him a sandwich from a COSTA café as he had no breakfast prepared for him.

When I saw that he was settled, I finally went to work. About 3pm I started calling him to check that he was alright. For the next two hours I called him about six times. I was worried but I thought maybe his daughter had come home and taken him out.

At about 5pm when I called again, his daughter answered the phone and said she had walked in from work to find him on the floor. He had fallen down and she could not lift him off the floor.

I went with my husband to pick him up off the floor. His daughter said she had called an ambulance and also added that he had fallen down over the weekend as well.

He was admitted to hospital that night and the next day I learnt he'd had a mild stroke over the weekend.

Professor Lynch was in hospital for about five weeks. I went to visit him an average of five times per week. I managed my work hours around the times I would go and see him. And I only missed a visit if I had to travel or a family situation came up.

I made sure I was there for lunch times because he could not feed himself properly and I wanted to make sure he did not make a mess and he ate with dignity. I made sure he was changed when he needed to be, checked on his clothing, kept the information line with his daughter open to ensure he had what he needed and befriended the nurses who took care of him. I took them a box of chocolates when he was discharged because they accommodated my many, tiresome requests.

A lot of times I'd walk in and his eyes would light up and he would say to the nurses *'That's my favourite'*.

On the second day of his admission to hospital he went to sleep and just refused to wake up. That was distressing to see and I cried worried that he would die. Even when the nurses said he would pull through I could not believe it as he looked so bad. When the doctor resuscitated him, he told the doctor *'you should have let me go.'*

The Professor was giving up because he was lonely, he was a man of great intellect and ability and skill and energy and now he found himself chair-bound, housebound, with very little human interaction except with BBC news on his television set.

He spent Christmas in hospital on his own. His daughters visited him in the morning and then he had his hospital Christmas lunch by himself. I had asked Emily if she was doing anything for him on Christmas day and she said yes, she and her sisters were coming to spend it with him.

It was something else to see a man of his calibre and contribution spend Christmas day in hospital alone without family and friends.

I nominated Professor Lynch for an award at the Gathering of Africa's Best. I sent a text to Emily, his daughter to ask her if she or any of her other three siblings would be happy to pick it up on their father's behalf. She said 'no' and suggested the Award be posted instead. So,

Professor Lynch was often featured in the press

I said *'never mind, I'll pick it up'*.

Professor Lynch was discharged from hospital after Christmas.

By January 11th 2020, I was happy with the final edit. The cover, forward and all the photographs and certificates were in place and I was ready to publish.

I was not interested in waiting for a publisher as the only positive responses I had had were charging me to publish. I'd set myself a commitment and a deadline to publish Professor Lynch's book and I was going to keep it. So, I decided to self-publish.

I chose a launch date, booked the venue, produced the invitations, went to Sierra Leone, his place of birth and booked a second launch there. I met the President and the First Lady who promised to support the book launch in Sierra Leone.

I came to realise that the children, led by the son were not happy I was writing his autobiography. Josh, the son wanted me to remove the book from Amazon due to what he called numerous mistakes and inaccuracies. He listed spelling mistakes and cited the name of his college as wrong. I immediately withdrew the book from Amazon and made those changes.

He then demanded several other changes which would negate the story that I had been told by Professor Lynch from his own mouth and recorded on video. I did not want to make those additional changes. In fact, one of the doctor's friends referred to this as 'engineering' the book.

So here I was shocked, disappointed, fifteen months of my life's work, time, energy, heart and soul on the floor. What was I going to do?

I could drop the book or I could carry on and re-write and publish It.

I had set out to tell a story, so, I was determined to do just that. And I set to work writing an Unofficial Biography.

Spending those past fifteen months with Professor Lynch has taught me a lot of things:

First, he had titled his original autobiography *'Work Conquers All.*

But I question that statement. Here is a man who worked hard, who committed his life to the service of others and for what? A small flat in Milton Keynes and no recognition from the people, hospital and country for whom he worked so hard.

One of the Chief Executives of Milton Keynes Hospital described him as *'one of the rocks on which the hospital has been built'*.

Marcus Setchell described him as a *'giant'* He added *'Chris Lynch has made an absolutely outstanding, internationally important contribution not just from his B-Lynch stitch but from focusing the world onto the problem of post-partum haemorrhage'.*

One of the things the professor told me was that he was disappointed the UK had not recognised his work. This great man now sits all day in front of the TV barely able to help himself with little to show for all he was and for all that he gave and did.

How then does Work Conquer All?

THE AUTHOR

Nana Ofori-Atta Oguntola is a filmmaker and producer who loves to tell stories, especially stories of under-represented people and groups.

She holds a BA Hons degree in TV, Drama and Theatre Studies from the University of Winchester and an Executive MBA in the Creative Industries from Ashridge Business School, HULT.

Her passion is telling stories that inspire other people to be and do better and above all to believe in their dreams.

She has produced a large catalogue of film and TV content and runs a training organisation in media and filmmaking. She provides consultancies in film and TV production and provides training for producers.

Her second book is 'Mine To Give' a book telling the stories of survivors of sexual violence and calling for governments and societies to do better to protect women and girls.

Her passion for Professor Lynch's story to reach other people has driven this project from start to finish.

CONNECT WITH NANA

in Nana Oguntola EMBACI

@ nanaoforiattaoguntola

🐦 NanaAmaOguntola

✉ nanaooguntola@gmail.com

nanaoguntola.me

Printed in Great Britain
by Amazon

24094767R00056